The Rockwool Foundation Research Unit

Estimating the Effect of Emigration from Poland on Polish Wages

Christian Dustmann, Tommaso Frattini
and Anna Rosso

University Press of Southern Denmark
Odense 2012

Estimating the Effect of Emigration from Poland on Polish Wages

Study Paper No. 43

Published by:
© The Rockwool Foundation Research Unit and University Press of Southern Denmark

Copying from this book is permitted only within institutions that have agreements with CopyDan, and only in accordance with the limitations laid down in the agreement

Address:
The Rockwool Foundation Research Unit
Sølvgade 10, 2nd floor
DK-1307 Copenhagen K

Telephone	+45 33 34 48 00
Fax	+45 33 34 48 99
E-mail	forskningsenheden@rff.dk
Home page	www.rff.dk

ISBN 978-87-90199-71-5
ISSN 0908-3979
October 2012
Print run: 350
Printed by: Specialtrykkeriet Viborg

Price: 60.00 DKK, including 25% VAT

Contents

1. Introduction 6

2. Background, data and descriptive 8
   2.1 Emigration from Poland 8
   2.2 The Data 9
   2.3 Sample and Variable Construction 11
   2.4 Descriptive Evidence 13
3. Theoretical and empirical framework 16
   3.1 The model 16
   3.2 Empirical implementation 18
   3.3 Internal Migration and Composition Effects 19
   3.4 Non-Random Emigration and Instrumental Variables estimation ... 21

4. Results 26
   4.1 Main findings 26
   4.2 Additional Results and Robustness Checks 28

5. Discussion and Conclusions 29

References 30

A Data Appendix 35
   A.1 Sample extraction 35
   A.2 The weights: estimation strategy 36
   A.3 Net and gross wages 36
   A.4 Missing wages 37
   A.5 Emigrant share 37

B The Theoretical Model 39
   B.1 Wage Determination: CES Production 39
   B.2 First order effect of emigration on the wage distribution 40
   *B.3 First order effect of emigration on the mean wages of
          the total population* 42
   B.4 First order Taylor expansion around m=0 42

C The Polish Economy and the Polish labour market 43

Tables 45

Figures 57

Estimating the Effect of Emigration from Poland on Polish Wages

Christian Dustmann°, Tommaso Frattini§ and Anna Rosso°

°*University College London and CReAM* §*Università degli Studi di Milano, CReAM, LdA and IZA*
October 2012

Abstract:

This paper contributes to a small but growing literature that studies the effects emigration has on the labour markets of the sending countries, focussing on Poland for the period 1998-2007. We develop a simple model that guides our empirical specification, and provides a clear interpretation for our estimates. The data we use is unique, in that it contains information about household members who are currently living abroad, allowing us to develop region specific emigration rates, and to estimate the effect emigration has on wages, using within-region variation. We also provide IV estimates, using information on labour market shocks in the largest destination countries as instruments. Our results show that emigration from Poland was largest for workers with intermediate skill levels, and that it is wages for this skill group that increased most. We also show that emigration led to a slight overall increase in wages. Workers at the low end of the skill distribution did not gain, but may have experienced slight wage decreases.

JEL-code: J31, J61
Keywords: Emigration, Wages, Impact.

* Financial support from the Rockwool Foundation is gratefully acknowledged. We thank the Foundation's Research Unit for their support, constructive comments, and productive collaboration during the project. We also wish to thank Iga Magda for her invaluable help with the data and Orazio Attanasio, David Card, Ian Preston, Florian Hoffmann, Thomas Lemieux, Uta Schoenberg, and participants to the CReAM-NORFACE Conference "Migration: Economic Change, Social Challenge", and to seminars at the University of British Columbia and the University of Bologna for their constructive comments.

1. Introduction

Since the late 1990's, Poland has experienced a dramatic increase in emigration. While in 1998, the share of emigrants on the overall population was about 0.50%, it increased to 2.3% only a decade later[1]. There is large regional variation in emigration rates, with the share of emigrants varying between 1 and 5.6 percent by 2007 across Poland's 16 provinces (Table 2). The composition of the emigration flow changed as well over this decade: Emigrants became increasingly younger and were better educated than non-emigrants. The large increases in emigration, and the variation in the skill composition of emigrants, are likely to have had an impact on the Polish labour market and – in particular – on the wages of those who stayed behind. It is this question that we address in this paper.

We investigate the wage impact of emigration over a period of ten years, between 1998 and 2007, a phase when emigration from Poland was largest. The approach we take in this paper is based on detailed information we have on emigrants, and their education and age structure, which allows us to assign emigration rates to local labour markets, and to determine the change in the skill ratios within local labour markets that is induced by emigration. Thus, the effects of emigration on wages of non-emigrants can be identified using variation of emigration rates within regions of Poland.

Our paper is related to the literature on the impact of migration on wages. While most studies concentrate on the wage impacts in the countries of destination[2], only a few papers exist that study the impact of emigration on the labour markets of sending countries. One reason for the lack of evidence on the effects of emigration on labour markets in the countries of origin is the difficulty in obtaining information on emigrants. Aydemir and Borjas (2007) and Mishra (2007) exploit the fact that over 95% of Mexican emigrants go to the US, and measure the size and composition of Mexican emigrants from US Censuses, and wages in Mexico from Mexican Censuses. They then follow the identification strategy proposed by Borjas (2003) and correlate wages of different skill groups, defined in terms of age and education, in Mexico, to the proportion of emigrants from the same skill group in the US. The concentration of Mexican emigrants in one only destination country provides an almost unique opportunity for studies of this kind. Elsner (2010) uses a similar approach to the study of Lithuanian emigration, but he has to

---

1 See Table 1.
2 See for instance early work by Altonji and Card (1991), Angrist and Kugler (2003), Card (2001), Borjas (2003), Card and Lewis (2007) and Dustmann, Fabbri and Preston (2005), Jaeger (2007) and more recent papers by D'Amuri, Ottaviano and Peri (2010), Dustmann, Frattini and Preston (2012), Glitz (2011), Manacorda, Manning and Wadsworth (2012), Ottaviano and Peri (2012).

rely on a number of simplifying assumptions to reconstruct the size of Lithuanian emigration based on Irish and UK data[3].

We contribute to this literature by focussing on a large European country, Poland, which was locked away behind the iron curtain for more than four decades, but experienced large emigration from the late 1990's onwards. While the aforementioned studies rely on Census and Survey information of the *destination* countries to identify emigrants, we have available detailed information about all emigrants, their age, and their education, which is measured in the emigration country, and which allows us to compute precisely the regional distribution of emigrants in the origin country. Further, availability of wage information on a subset of emigrants before they left the country helps us to address the possible change in composition in the non-emigrant population, due to selective out-migration.

To better structure our empirical analysis and to interpret our parameter estimates, we present first a model where output is produced by combining capital with a CES labour composite. The model shows that wage effects are positive for those skill groups where out-migration is above a weighted overall average along the skill distribution, and that – for capital being insufficiently mobile in the short run – overall wage effects can be expected to be positive. We show that emigration from Poland over the period from 1998 to 2007 became increasingly skilled, with the highest fraction of emigrants among those with an intermediate level of education. Our empirical results, based on estimation which uses the variation within regions, suggest that emigration had – overall – a positive effect on the wages of those who did not emigrate. Across skill groups, it is particularly those in the middle of the educational distribution that experienced the largest gains from emigration. This is in line with our theoretical model, which suggests this group as the main beneficiary of Polish out-migration. The effect on the highly educated is likewise positive, but smaller in magnitude, while the effect on wages of the low educated is slightly negative, although mostly not significantly different from zero. This is in line with emigration being more concentrated among individuals in the middle and the upper part of the educational distribution. Within the simple model that we develop, these results indicate also that the capital stock in Poland has been inelastic in the short run, which explains the positive overall effect.

---

3 Other papers on the labour market effects of emigration include: Hanson (2007) who studies Mexico, comparing changes in labour market outcomes between 1990 and 2000 in Mexican states with high and low historical level of migration (measured in the 1950s); Docquier, Ozden and Peri (2011) who use an aggregate production function model to simulate the effect of immigration and emigration on wages and employment in OECD countries; Elsner (2011) who uses a calibrated structural model of labor demand to simulate the effect of Lithuanian emigration on wages of non-emigrant workers.

As emigration from a particular region may be induced by negative wage shocks, such estimates constitute a lower bound on the effect emigration has on wages, and have therefore a meaningful interpretation. To further address this selection problem, we develop an IV estimation strategy, which is based on detailed information we have available about destination countries of emigrants. We combine this with the variation of economic conditions in the main destination countries (Ireland, Germany, the UK and the US) over this period, as well as the large exchange rate fluctuations, and employ various strategies that exploit regional differences in destination preferences. Our IV results lead to similar conclusions.

The structure of the paper is as follows. In the next section, we describe the data, emigrants' main characteristics and briefly give an overview of the Polish economy over the period of analysis. In section 3, we explain the theoretical model and our identification strategy. Section 4 presents the OLS and IV results, and show several robustness checks. Section 5 discusses the results and concludes.

2. Background, data and descriptive

2.1 Emigration from Poland

The first large-scale migrations from Poland happened towards the end of the Nineteenth century. Sluggish economic development and large population growth led to many Poles looking for better opportunities in other countries, and this trend intensified during the interwar period. Between 1919 and 1938, about one million people emigrated permanently to the USA, France and Brazil (Zubrzycki, 1953), and circulatory migration took place to Germany and Latvia. Emigration slowed down after the great depression in the 1930's. In the period after WWII, emigration from Poland increased again, mainly due to political motives. Between 1950 and 1992, more than two million Poles left the country (see Fassmann et al., 1994). Over this period, a large fraction of emigrants moved to the United States[4].

After 1989, the year of the fall of the Berlin wall, emigration from Poland was initially relatively modest, up to the late 1990's, due to relatively favourable economic conditions in Poland. It began to increase steadily from about 1998 onwards, coinciding with a slowdown in GDP growth, and a decrease in employment, and peaked in 2007. We provide information about the overall recent emigration trends from Poland in Figure 1 and more details in Table 1. Entries in the Table and the Figure are based on data from the Polish Labour Force Survey

---

4 As pointed out by Mostwin (1969), most of the Polish immigration to the USA after the Second World War was due to political motives. Compared to earlier immigrants from Poland to the US, those who arrived after WWII were better educated.

(PLFS), where observations are weighted using population weights (see below for details). The Figure shows that the number of emigrants is just above 100,000 in 1998, and increases to more than 600,000 in 2007. The stock of emigrants nearly quintupled between 1998 and 2007, and slightly decreased from 2007 to 2008, due to the economic crisis, which severely affected the main destination countries.

In 2004, Poland became a member of the European Union, and its citizens had the right to travel freely across all EU member states. In addition, the UK, Sweden and Ireland allowed Polish citizens full access to their labour markets, while the other EU countries took advantage of a seven year transition arrangement, under which Poles were refused the right to work in these countries. However, this was not strictly imposed by all countries; for instance, Germany gave (on a case to case basis) many Poles access to its labour market[5]. This led to annual increases in the number of emigrants by between 20 and 40 percent in the years after 2004 (see Kaczmarczyk and Okólski (2008) and Kaczmarczyk, Mioduszewska, and Zylicz (2009) for details on post-accession Polish emigration).

2.2 The Data

The Polish Labour Force Survey (PLFS)

The main dataset we use for our analysis is the Polish Labour Force Survey (PLFS), and we focus on the period between 1998 and 2007. The PLFS is a rotating quarterly panel of about 15,000 households, or 50,000 individuals for each quarter, where each household is interviewed four times, and it is conducted by the Polish Central Statistical Office (GUS) in all the 16 provinces[6] (*voivodeships*) of Poland. Individuals are interviewed for two consecutive quarters, and then again for two consecutive quarters after a gap of two quarters. Thus, the entire interview period spans 1½ years.

---

5 The number of Poles resident in Germany increased between 1995 and 2003, decreased dramatically (by 10%) in 2004 when Germany was substituted by those European countries that allowed Poles access to their labour market after Poland's EU accession, but started to increase again reaching previous levels in 2005. After 2004, the number of working permits issued to first time Polish employee in Germany was 15,092 in 2006 and increasing to 17,312 in 2007 (see German Federal Employment Agency, http://statistik.arbeitsagentur.de/Navigation/Statistik/Statistik-nachThemen/Beschaeftigung/Arbeitsgenehmigungen-Zustimmungen/Arbeitsgenehmigungen-ZustimmungenNav.html). An administrative measure of immigration flows into the UK can be obtained from the Worker Registration Scheme. Between May 2004 and March 2007, 394,180 Poles registered to work in the country (Home Office, 2009). These figures are higher than the numbers we have from the UK LFS as immigrants are not forced to de-register from the scheme if they leave the country, thus they only capture gross inflows.
6 See Appendix for a more detailed description of the sample used.

The survey covers all individuals aged 15 and above, and who are living in the same household. The PLFS provides information on demographic, personal and household characteristics of all interviewed individuals, which include age, education, current and past region of residence, country of birth, number of children. It also has detailed information on the economic activity of each member of the household during the week preceding the interview. This covers employment status, work arrangements, occupation, industry, and monthly net wages. Moreover, and important for our analysis, information is also collected about individuals who are part of the household but who have been residing abroad for more than three months. The information collected on these individuals includes their age, their education level, the region where they come from, the relationship with other members of the household, and their country of present residence. This information allows us to construct a measure of out-migration, where we know the detailed demographic characteristics of the emigrants. The survey also provides population weights for the resident population. We use these throughout the analysis, and we also use these weights to reconstruct population weights for emigrants. We give details on how we do this in the Appendix A.2.

Other Data Sets

In addition to the PLFS, we also use microdata for Germany, the UK and the US and aggregated data for Ireland (the four main countries of destination for Polish emigrants) for some parts of the analysis. In particular, we use these data to cross-check the validity of emigration measures in the PLFS (see below), and to construct our instrumental variables (see section 3) which are based on the wage growth in destination countries.

Information for Germany comes from the IAB Employment History Data, a dataset of administrative social security records available for years 1975-2007. The data is made up of all individuals covered by the social security system, which is about 80% of the German workforce, including all workers who are subject to social security contributions (excluding self-employed and public employees). Immigrants in this dataset can only be identified based on their nationality, as there is no information on country of birth. For the UK, we rely on the UK Labour Force Survey, a quarterly rotating panel survey available in its current format since 1992, with rich demographic and labour market information, including gross wages, country of birth and years since migration. Data for the US come from the IPUMS-CPS (Integrated Public Use Microdata Series of the March Current Population Survey), an integrated dataset of 48 years (1962-2009) of the March Current Population Survey (CPS). The CPS is a monthly household survey which contains information on labour market status and demographics, including country of birth and years since migration. As neither the Irish Labour Force Survey, nor on any other Irish microdata contain information on wages, we use aggregate wage information for Ireland that is provided by the Central Statistical Office, reporting weekly earnings by industrial sector, gender and type of employee. This data are based on the Earnings Hours and Employment Costs Survey (EHECS), which covers all sectors of the economy other than Agriculture, Forestry and Fishing (NACE 5-96). It is a quarterly survey using a sample of 7500 enterprises that report information on the number of employees, hours, earnings, bonuses in the quarter.

2.3 Sample and Variable Construction

We use the PLFS for the years between 1998 and 2007 to construct the two key variables for our analysis: emigration rates, by region and time period; and wages of non-emigrants, by region, time period, and educational group. We restrict our analysis to the age group between 15 and 65 years.

Emigration Rates

A strength of the PLFS is that it reports information on household members who are emigrants. When an individual who was a household member is not present, another member of the household is asked about the whereabouts of this person. If the individual has emigrated abroad more than three months earlier[7], detailed information on age, education, country of emigration and the role in the household of that individual is collected in a separate questionnaire. This information allows measuring directly the individual characteristics of emigrants, which is a main advantage over other studies that rely on destination country information to characterise emigrants. We use this information to construct emigration rates. In 857 cases, we observe individuals who are originally in the country, but emigrate over the sampling period. For this subsample of individuals, we have therefore the full set of information including their wage and occupation in Poland before emigration, in addition to the standard information on emigrants. We use this information in section 3.3 to analyse selection patterns among emigrants, based on comparison on their residual wages with those of non-emigrants.

One drawback of computing emigration rates based on this data is that by construction, emigrants who lived in single households are omitted, as are households where everybody emigrates at the same time. This leads to a potential undercount of emigrants. However, the percentage of people living in single households in Poland is relatively small, between 8% and 9% on average, has remained fairly constant over the years, and is similar across regions. In contrast, the same share was about 18% in the UK in 2007. Moreover, single households

---

7 Individuals abroad for less than three months are not recorded as emigrants, and cannot be separately identified in the data.

are far more frequent among the elderly: while the share of individuals living in single households is over 15% for the age group between 50 and 64 and about 8% for the age group 40-50, it is less than 7% for the age group between 25 and 40, which is the age group that accounts for about half of all emigrants. We provide in Section 4.2 additional robustness checks where we reconstruct the share of emigrants in the regional population, by assuming that within groups defined by year, region, age and education, the share of single households in the emigrant population corresponds the share of single households in the non-emigrant population, which we do observe (see Appendix A.5 for details).

To assess the emigration data computed on the basis of the PLFS, we use destination-country data to compare the trends in immigrant inflows into each country with the trend in emigration from the PLFS to that particular country. We focus on the three main destination countries of Polish emigrants: Germany, the UK, and the US. These three countries alone account for over 55% of all Polish immigration over the years we consider. In Figure 2 we plot the evolution of the stock of Polish immigrants in Germany, the UK, and the US, as estimated from German, UK and US microdata (solid line) and from the PLFS (scattered line)[8]. The estimates from these independent datasets are re-assuring similar, showing very similar trends across data sources. We have also computed the 95 percent confidence interval for the difference in the two data series. For Germany, the difference between the two estimates is only statistically significant in the first three years (despite very precise estimates for the German series, due to the large number of observations); for the UK, the difference is statistically significant only in 2007. The differences in estimates of Polish immigrants between the CPS and the PLFS are never statistically significant. Overall, these figures suggest that the emigration data we are using are quite accurate.

The share of emigrants on the total working age Polish population increased from 0.50 percent in 1998 to 2.29 percent in 2007[9]. This is a dramatic increase. At the same time there was substantial variation in emigration rates across the different regions, and into the different destination countries. We illustrate this in Table 2: for some regions, the share of emigrants over the working age population increased more than tenfold between 1998 and 2007 (Lower Silesian), while for other

---

[8] We use the IABS, UK LFS and CPS data for Germany, the UK and the US, respectively. See section 2.2 for details on these datasets. Since the UK LFS and CPS have information on years since migration, we can in this case focus on recent emigrants, and in the figure we plot the number of Poles who have been in the UK or the US for less than two years. For the US data, measurement of Polish immigrants is noisy due to small sample sizes. In the figure, we smooth the graph by using a 3 years moving average.

[9] The emigration share is computed as the number of emigrants at time t over the working age population (emigrants + residents) in the same year t.

regions it increased by less than 80% (e.g Podlaskie). The 2007 share of emigrants ranges between 0.9% (Masovian) and almost 6% (Subcarpathian). The Table also shows that the destination countries have changed over the period. While Germany was the main destination in 1997, absorbing about 27% of the Polish emigrant population, the largest destination country in 2007 is the UK (with 31% of all emigrants). Again, there is some substantial variation across regions in the destinations emigrants choose.

Wages

The measure on wages that is available in the PLFS is monthly net wages, i.e. gross wages after deduction of income taxes and social security taxes. For the construction of our wage variable (which we compute by region/year), we pool all quarters within a year. We restrict the sample to the working age population (15-65), and we drop the top and bottom wage percentile to eliminate outliers. We also eliminate all individuals who changed their migration status during the survey period so that regional mean wages within a calendar year are always computed for the non-emigrant population only, minimising changes in wages due to changes in the sample composition. Over the period we consider, real net wages increase on average by 1.7% per year.

Poland has a progressive taxation system, and the tax schedule is constant across regions, although it varies over time. Based on information about the taxation rules and the information that is available about the household (see Appendix A.3 for details), we compute gross wages, and re-estimate our model to check robustness of our results.

The response rate to the wage question in the PLFS has decreased over our observation window, with non-response being higher for the highly educated (non-response in 1998 was below 20% for all education groups; however, by 2007, it has increased to 22% for the low educated, 29% for individuals with an intermediate education, and to 40% for those with high education group). In order to check whether this affects our results, we correct wages by imputing them for those who report they are employed but do not report their salary (see Appendix A.4 for the procedure we use).

2.4 Descriptive Evidence

Emigrants and Non-Emigrants

How do emigrants differ from non-emigrants? In Table 3, we report the average characteristics of emigrants and non-emigrants for the years 1998 and 2007. The figures in the table show that emigrants in both years are substantially younger than non-emigrants, with the average age for emigrants decreasing by about 2 years between 1998 and 2007. Furthermore, emigrants are far better educated. We define three education levels, low intermediate, and high, based on individuals' qualifications. Specifically, we classify as "low education" individuals who have at most lower secondary education, or up to 8 years of schooling; we classify as "intermediate education" individuals with secondary education, or between 9 and 13 years of schooling, and as "high education" individuals with postsecondary or tertiary education, or more than 13 years of schooling[10]. For both years, the fraction of individuals with low education is lower in the population of emigrants, while the fraction of those with intermediate education is higher. The overall share of individuals with low education decreased substantially between 1998 and 2007 for both emigrants and non-emigrants, with the drop being even larger for emigrants. These figures suggest that emigrants are over-represented among the intermediate and highly educated, but underrepresented among the low educated.

Are these numbers similar for the different regions, and across time periods? We illustrate this graphically in Figure 3, where we plot (for all years and all regions) the share of each education group in the emigrant population against the share of each education group in the overall population. If the skill composition of the emigrant population was identical to that of the overall population, then all dots would lie on the 45 degree line. The figure shows clearly that this is not the case: for most region-year pairs, the share of the intermediately and – to a lesser extent – highly educated is higher among emigrants than among the overall population. In contrast, the share of individuals with low education is clearly lower among emigrants than in the overall population. These numbers suggest that emigration led to a decrease in the share of the medium and highly educated, but to a relative increase in the share of the low educated. We discuss the consequences this should have on wages of non-emigrants in the next section.

Destination Countries

How are emigrants to the different destination countries selected along the education distribution? In the first column of Table 4 we report the share of Polish emigrants living in Germany, Ireland[11], the UK, and the US, and, overall, in a EU27[12] country, for the years 1998 and 2007. We report these figures for all Polish emigrants, and for those who emigrated within the last year (recent emigrants). In 1998, almost one third of all Polish emigrants lived in the US, just under 30% in

---

10 See Appendix A1 for a detailed explanation on the original classification in the Polish LFS.
11 According to the Polish LFS there are no emigrants to Ireland in 1998.
12 In Appendix Table A1 we break down the percentage of emigrants residing in each of the European countries.

Germany, and only 5% in the UK; further, the new flows of emigrants were mostly directed toward Germany (36%), and to a lesser extent the US (15%), with only 6% of new emigrants going to the UK, and no emigration to Ireland. However, by 2007 the situation has reversed: one third of Polish emigrants live now in the UK, 18% in Germany, 12% in Ireland, and only 6% in the US. This is a reflection of a sharp change in the destination of emigration flows: in 2007, 37% of new Polish emigrants choose the UK as a destination, 12% Ireland, 16% Germany, and only 3% move to the US. Overall, 88% of all new Polish emigrants in 2007 move to a EU country. By 2007, 84% of all Polish emigrants live in a EU country, up from 55% in 1998. Destination countries differ greatly in the composition of their Polish immigrant population: we report the distribution of immigrants across education groups in each destination country in columns 2-4. In column 5 we show the average age of emigrants in the different countries. Emigrants to Germany and the US are older and lower educated (especially those to the US), emigrants to the UK and Ireland are far younger, with a higher share of intermediate and highly educated. While the average age of emigrants in the US has remained stable over the years, emigrants to Germany became older, especially if compared to the average age of the total emigrant population.

Emigrant Households

Which are the households that send emigrants? In Table 5 we report results from running simple regressions on the probability that a household is home to an emigrant. The last two columns show the means of the variables we use in the regression. We condition on the standardised average earnings in the household (computed as the mean among the wage earners, e.g. if there are 4 family members but only 2 of them receive a salary, the average is computed among the two earners)[13], the number of household members, the share of intermediate and highly educated, share of women, the average age in the household (divided by 100), and the percentage of employed older than 25 (to avoid including individuals who are still in education) in the household. In all cases, we control for year, quarter and region dummies. All variables except earnings and employment status are constructed including emigrant household members too. Households who send emigrants tend to have lower average wages, are larger, and have a lower share of household members with low education than households with no emigrants. On average, there are less women in emigrants' households, and the average age is three years younger.

In column (1), we condition on the full set of explanatory variables, thus reporting the conditional associations of household characteristics with the probability that the household is home to an emigrant. This probability is negatively associated

---

13 Emigrants do not receive any salary, but they are counted as members of the family.

with mean family earnings, and positively associated with the number of household members. Thus, emigrants are from larger households, and from households where the average earnings of those who work are lower. Further, the probability that a household is home to an emigrant increases with the education level of the household: The higher is the share of intermediate and high educated in a household, the higher the probability that the household has a member residing abroad. In column (2) we do not control for the share of education and in column (3) we do not control for the share of employed within the household, this does not affect the results.

3. Theoretical and empirical framework

3.1 The model

We next develop a model that helps us to interpret the parameters that we estimate, drawing on work by Dustmann, Frattini and Preston (2012). Assume that the number of output types (output being denoted by y) is equal to one, and that there are multiple labour types, $i=1,...,L^{14}$. In our analysis below, we will distinguish labour types by their skill levels. We normalise the price of y to 1.

We adopt a nested CES production function, producing output y by combing a labour composite H with capital K:

$$y = \left[\beta H^s + (1-\beta)K^s\right]^{1/s} \qquad (1)$$

where H is a CES aggregate of the different labour types li, $H = \left[\sum_i \alpha_i l_i^\sigma\right]^{1/\sigma}$, and α_i determines the productivity of the ith type of labour. The elasticity of substitution between labour types is determined by $\sigma \leq 1$, β determines the relative productivity of labour and capital, and $s \leq 1$ determines the elasticity of substitution between capital and labour.

We assume that emigrant and non-emigrant labour of the same type are both perfect substitutes and equally productive, so that non-emigrant labour of type i, l_i, is the difference between labour before migration l_i^0, and emigrant labour, l_i^1: $l_i = l_i^0 - l_i^1$. For the markets for each labour type to clear, $l_i = n_i$ for all i, where n_i is the supply of labour of the ith type. The labour supply n_i is then the difference between labour supply in the particular skill group before emigration n_i^0, and emigrants n_i^1, so that $n_i = n_i^0 - n_i^1$. It follows that $n_i = N(\pi_i^0 - \pi_i^1 m)$ where $N =$

---

14 Thus, the model excludes adjustment to labour supply shocks other than through factor prices, as discussed for instance, in Quispe-Agnoli and Zavodny (2002), Hanson and Slaughter (2002), Lewis (2003, 2011), Gandal, Hanson and Slaughter (2004), Dustmann and Glitz (2011), and Gonzalez and Ortega (2011).

$\sum_i n_i^0$ is total (pre-migration) labour supply, $\pi_i^0 = n_i^0 / N$ is the fraction of total labour supply of the ith type, $\pi_i^1 = n_i^1 / \sum_j n_j^1$ is the fraction of emigrant labour of the ith type and $m = \sum_j n_j^1 / N$ is the ratio of emigrants to the total (pre-migration) labour force. First order conditions for profit-maximising input choice imply that the real wage of the ith type of labour, w_i, equals its marginal product. Similarly, the price of capital, ρ, equals the marginal product of capital. Deriving the first order condition and taking logs results in an expression for equilibrium real wages of all labour types (and equivalently for capital K):

$$\ln w_i = \ln \frac{\partial y}{\partial l_i} =$$

$$= \ln \beta \alpha_i + (\sigma - 1)\ln(\pi_i^0 - \pi_i^1 m) + (1-\sigma)\ln\left(\frac{H}{N}\right) + \left(\frac{1}{s}-1\right)\ln\left[\beta + (1-\beta)\left(\frac{K}{H}\right)^s\right] \quad (2)$$

where $\ln\left(\dfrac{H}{N}\right) = \dfrac{1}{\sigma}\ln\left(\sum_j \alpha_j (\pi_j^0 - \pi_j^1 m)^\sigma\right)$

To derive the effect that emigration has on wages for the different skill groups of non-emigrants, and on the mean wage, suppose an elasticity of supply of capital given by $\theta = \dfrac{\partial \ln K}{\partial \ln \rho}$.

Then the equilibrium change in native log wages as a reaction to changes in the emigrant-native ratio can be shown to be (see Appendix B for details):

$$\left.\frac{d\ln w_i}{dm}\right|_{m=0} = (1-\sigma)\left(\frac{\pi_i^1}{\pi_i^0} - \phi\sum \omega_j \frac{\pi_j^1}{\pi_j^0}\right) \quad (3)$$

where ω_i is the contribution of the ith type to the labour aggregate H^σ, with $\sum_i \omega_i = 1$, ψ is the contribution of labour to the overall CES aggregate y^s, and ϕ is a parameter that depends on capital mobility θ, capital-labour substitutability s and the labour share ψ. Notice that (4) implies that the pattern of the effects of emigration on each skill-specific wage of non emigrants depends upon the relative density of emigrants and non-emigrants $\dfrac{\pi_i^1}{\pi_i^0}$ at that skill type.

Consider first the case $\phi = 1$, which arises (assuming that capital and labour are not perfectly substitutable, $s \neq 1$, and the capital share is not equal to zero, $\psi \neq 1$) if capital is perfectly mobile ($\theta=\infty$).[15] Since $\sum \omega_i = 1$, the rightmost expression in parentheses in (3) is the difference for that skill type between the relative density of emigrants and total labour supply, and a weighted average of these relative densities across the skill distribution. The wage of any skill type is increased by emigration if and only if the intensity of emigration at that point exceeds an appropriately weighted average of emigration intensity across all skills types. If the distribution of skill types in the emigrant outflow exactly matches that in the total labour force (before emigration), $\pi_i^0 = \pi_i^1$ for all i, and the effect on wages is everywhere zero.

If capital is used, imperfectly mobile and imperfectly substitutable with labour, then $\phi<1$. In this case, even emigration which matches the native labour force in composition, will result in wage gains, as $\pi_i^1 / \pi_i^0 > \phi \sum \omega_j (\pi_j^1/\pi_j^0)$. The pattern of wage effects along the distribution will be driven in just the same way by the relative density of emigrants and natives $\dfrac{\pi_i^1}{\pi_i^0}$.

The effect of emigration on mean native wages $\sum_i w_i \pi_i^0$, also derived in the Appendix, is

$$\left.\dfrac{d \ln w_i}{dm}\right|_{m=0} = (1-\sigma)(1-\phi)\overline{w}^0 \sum_i \omega_i \dfrac{\pi_i^1}{\pi_i^0} \geq 0 \qquad (4)$$

where $\overline{w}^0$ is the mean wage before emigration. If capital is perfectly mobile so that $\phi =1$, then this effect is zero.[16] That does not, of course, mean that in this case wage changes are zero at for all skill types. Wages increase at any point in the distribution at which $\dfrac{\pi_i^1}{\pi_i^0}$ 1 exceeds the weighted average $\sum_i \omega_i \dfrac{\pi_i^1}{\pi_i^0}$, as we explain above.

3.2 Empirical implementation

Taking a Taylor approximation of (2) around $m=0$ using (3), we obtain an estimable equation

$$\ln w_{irt} = a_{ir} + b_{it} + c_i X_{rt} + \beta_i m_{rt} + \varepsilon_{irt} \qquad (5),$$

---

15 This follows from $\phi = 1 + \dfrac{(1-s)(1-\psi)}{1+(1-s)\psi\theta} \dfrac{1}{(\sigma-1)}$, which is equal to 1 if capital is perfectly mobile ($\theta=\infty$).

16 See Dustmann, Frattini and Preston (2012) for more details, and for a derivation of the second order effects (the "migration surplus") in a similar context.

where $\ln w_{irt}$ are log mean wages of the non-emigrant population in skill group i, period t and region r, a_{ir} and b_{it} are region and time dummies, collecting terms that vary across regions and over time, and X_{rt} controls for changes in the age and skill composition of the overall labour force (see Dustmann et al. (2012) for more details). The parameter β_i corresponds to the term $(\sigma-1)[\pi_i^1 / \pi_i^0 - \phi \sum \omega_j (\pi_j^1 / \pi_j^0)]$ above, and measures the effect of emigration on wages of skill group i. In our empirical implementation we define skill groups as education groups. Our model provides a clear-cut prediction for our parameter estimates: when we regress wages for a particular skill group on the fraction of emigrants to the overall workforce, m_{it}, the sign of this parameter estimate will be positive (as $\sigma < 1$) if emigrants are more densely represented in that skill group than natives. Furthermore, this estimate is the larger, the smaller the short-run supply elasticity of capital. Finally, it follows from (4) that emigration will only have positive effect on average wages if the elasticity of capital supply is smaller than 1, so that capital is not perfectly mobile (at least in the short term).

We measure m_{it} as the ratio of emigrants in a particular region at a particular point in time to the total regional population before emigration: $m_{it} = Emigrants_{it} / (Emigrants_{it} + Residents_{it})$. The vector X_{it} collects additional control variables, which include average regional age, the ratios of the number of individuals with high and intermediated education to the number of low educated individuals in the region, and the logarithm of the total regional population. We provide detail on these variables in Table 6.

We estimate (5) by conditioning on region specific fixed effects, thus effectively identifying the impact of emigration on wages through variation in the emigration share (m_{it}) within regions and over time. We also control for year fixed effects. We use the years 1998-2007, and as regions the 16 Polish *voivodeships* (see Table 2). Thus, our data includes for each skill group 160 observation.

3.3 Internal Migration and Composition Effects

Internal migration

If regions that experience high international emigration are also receiving internal immigrants, then this would offset the effects of international emigration, and lead to an underestimate of the effect of emigration on wages. If instead the same regions that experience high international emigration, experience also emigration to other Polish regions, we would over-estimate the effect of international emigration on regional wages (see also Borjas, Freeman, and Katz, 1996 and 1997). The PLFS reports, since 2001, information on region of residence one year before the interview, which we can use to check the degree of internal migration across the different Polish regions, and how it is associated with international migration. Overall, internal mobility in Poland is low, and decreasing over time: in 2001 0.24% of the population reports to live in a different region than in the previous year, and this share has decreased to 0.12% in 2007. To check whether these internal movements are correlated with international emigration, we regress the share of internal migrants in the total regional population on the share of international emigrants, controlling for region fixed effects and time dummies. The resulting estimate is small, negative and not statistically significant (we estimate a coefficient of -0.041 with a standard error of 0.027). Further, regressing the share of internal migrants in each region and year on the share of international migrants by skill group (controlling for year and regional dummies) results again in estimates that are not significantly different from zero[17]. We have also run regressions along the lines of Card and DiNardo (2000), to check whether emigration does affect the proportion of the population in different skill groups, and found no evidence that the internal mobility decisions of individuals in a skill group are affected by the international emigration of individuals in the same skill group. We call NE_{rit} the non-emigrant population in region r with education i in period t and E_{rit} the emigrants in region r with education i in period t. Following Card and DiNardo we can define the relative growth rate of emigrants in education group i as $\left(\frac{\Delta E_{irt}}{NE_{irt-1}} - \frac{\Delta E_{rt}}{NE_{rt-1}} \right)$ and the relative growth rate of non-emigrants in education group i as $\left(\frac{\Delta NE_{irt}}{NE_{irt-1}} - \frac{\Delta NE_{rt}}{NE_{rt-1}} \right)$.

We can then run the following regression of the relative change in non-emigrants on the relative change of emigrants for each education group.

$$\left(\frac{\Delta NE_{irt}}{NE_{irt-1}} - \frac{\Delta NE_{rt}}{NE_{rt-1}} \right) = \alpha + \beta \left(\frac{\Delta E_{irt}}{NE_{irt-1}} - \frac{\Delta E_{rt}}{NE_{rt-1}} \right) + \gamma \left(\frac{\Delta NE_{irt-1}}{NE_{irt-2}} - \frac{\Delta NE_{rt-1}}{NE_{rt-2}} \right) + \delta \frac{\Delta NE_{rt}}{NE_{rt-1}} + \phi \frac{\Delta NE_{rt-1}}{NE_{rt-2}} + \xi_{irt}$$

In addition, we control for the relative growth rate in the non-emigrant population in the previous period (the lag of the dependent variable), the growth rate of the regional population between t and t-1 and the growth rate of the regional population in the previous period, in order to capture all the possible dynamics of the changes in the non-emigrants population. These variables allow us to control for pre-existing market conditions that could drive away individuals from the region (see Borjas et al., 1997). We report results of this regression in Table 7. In each panel of the table we show results of the regression of the relative growth

---

17 Our estimated coefficients (standard errors) are: -0.023 (0.028) for the low education group; -0.021 (0.027) for the intermediate education group; 0.006 (0.06) for the high education group.

rate in the non-emigrant population of low educated (Panel A), intermediate educated (Panel B) and high educated (Panel C) on the relative growth rate of emigrant population of the same education group for years 1998 to 2007. We would expect, in the emigration case, to have either a zero or a negative coefficient β, which would imply that non-emigrants do not move into those regions where emigration is higher. The results are confirmed: we see a negative, slightly significant coefficient for low educate in Panel A, but a coefficient close to zero and non significant for both intermediate and high educated.

Composition Effects

A further source of concern is the possibility that emigrants are not a random sample of the regional population within each skill group i. If migrants within skill group i are positively (negatively) selected, then average wages for Polish residents in skill group i can decrease (increase) after emigration, which would be purely a result of a composition effect.

In order to check if there is selection, we compare log-wage residuals of non-emigrants and emigrants, using the sample of 857 emigrants for which we have information on wages before emigration (see Section 2.3)[18]. The overall mean difference in residuals between emigrants and non-emigrants is not significantly different from zero, and neither are the mean differences by education group. To investigate this further, we plot the kernel density estimates of the residual distribution for emigrants and non-emigrants, reported in the left panel of Figure 4. In the right panel we plot the difference between the emigrant and the non-emigrant estimated densities at each percentile of the residual wage distribution (($f^E(p) - f^{NE}(p)$)), where $f(.)$ is the pdf of the residual distribution at each percentile p for emigrants and non-emigrants)[19]. The graph shows that the difference is not statistically significant at almost all percentiles.

3.4 Non-Random Emigration and Instrumental Variables estimation

A further potential problem with specification (5) is that emigration choices may not be random. Region fixed effects account for permanent regional differences, and therefore also for the fact that – for instance – emigration may be higher from rural regions, or from regions that are traditionally less wealthy. However, even

---

18 We compute residuals from a weighted log-wage regression on education (3 categories), age, age squared, occupation dummies for each 1-digit ISCO08 occupation group, region and year dummies.
19 Confidence intervals are estimated using the Stata command asciker (Fiorio, 2004), which computes the asymptotic confidence intervals for each point estimate in the kernel density, following Horowitz (2001) and Hall (1992).

after controlling for region fixed effects, it may still be the case that region specific shocks affecting wages of skill group i in year t (ε_{irt}) are correlated with regional emigration flows in the same year. In this case, our OLS estimates would be biased.

If emigration is higher from regions that experience negative wage shocks, which seems plausible, then this induces a spurious negative correlation between emigration and wage growth, which leads to a negative bias in the OLS estimate of the effect of emigration on mean wages. The OLS estimator will therefore provide a lower bound for the actual effect of emigration on mean wages. Moreover, the OLS estimator will be a lower bound for the effect of emigration on wages of each skill group i, as long as skill-specific shocks are positively correlated within regions in every year. We test this by running separate pairwise regressions of regional wage growth rates for each skill group on wage growth of all other skill groups, controlling for year dummies. In all cases, we find that growth rates of wages for all skill groups are positively correlated within regions, although the estimated coefficients are not significant for the correlation between wages of low and highly educated individuals[20].

Given the argument above, we can interpret our estimates on the effect of emigration on wages of non-emigrants as *lower* bounds. In addition, we use an IV strategy to predict the emigration rates across the different regions. This requires an instrument, or a set of instruments, that are correlated with m_{rt} – the ratio of emigrants over the total population in region r at time t – but uncorrelated with ε_{irt} – the economic shock hitting region r at time t, conditional on time-region dummies, and the set of individual characteristics that we include. Most of the literature that uses spatial variation to identify the effect of immigration on native outcomes uses an IV strategy that is based on the idea that past location choices of immigrants are not correlated with current region-specific shocks, which can therefore be used as predictors for immigrant inflows (see e.g. Altonji and Card (1991), Card (2001), Cortes (2008), Dustmann, Frattini and Preston (2012), Frattini (2008), Bianchi, Buonanno and Pinotti (2011)). In our case, Polish emigration before 1997 was too low to construct an equivalent instrument. Instead, we adopt an IV strategy that is based on economic shocks to destination countries, which are likely to influence emigration (testable), while being uncorrelated with the shocks to a particular Polish region (which is our identifying assumption). We allow the effect of destination countries' shocks on the probability of migration to differ across regions through regional heterogeneity in migration costs to each potential destination country.

---

20 We estimate a coefficient (standard error) of 0.898 (0.257) for the regression of low skilled wages on intermediate skilled wages; 0.196 (0.145) for the regression of low skilled wages on high skilled wages; 0.303 (0.148) for the regression of high skilled wages on intermediate skilled wages.

More precisely, let individuals' emigration decisions be driven by differences in expected wages between the home country (or the home region), and the destination countries. Economic shocks to each country of destination will have differential effects on emigration rates from different Polish regions. For instance, travel costs to the UK will differ across Polish regions depending on their proximity to airports with international flights, or on the size of the existing stock of emigrants from that region that already resides in the UK.

Emigration from regions with lower costs of emigration to the UK will react more to positively to positive shocks to the UK economy, while regions with, for example, lower emigration costs to Germany will be more sensitive to shocks to the German economy. We therefore use shocks to the main countries of destination of Polish emigrants as exogenous "pull factors" and allow them to have differential effects on different Polish regions using different weighting strategies. Further, we also use the discontinuity in Polish emigration following the 2004 entry of Poland in the EU. After the EU enlargement, Polish citizens gained the right of free movement to all EU countries, and free access to the labour market of Ireland, Sweden, and the UK. We utilise this variation in our identification strategy.

To implement this IV strategy, we use the four countries to which the majority of Polish emigrants migrated over the period we consider: Germany, Ireland, the UK and the US. On average, about 65% of emigrants settled in one of these four countries between 1998 and 2007. For each of these countries we define a variable Z_j which captures the attractiveness of the respective destination country j for potential migrants, and we use various measures for this. Each variable Z_j is expected to be correlated with the inflow of immigrants into country j, but should not be correlated with any shock specific to a particular Polish region. Notice that any possible correlations of Z_j with economic shocks that are common to all Polish regions are fully captured by the time dummies. Our exclusion restriction is that destination countries' shocks do not have region-specific consequences for Poland, apart from changing relative migration costs.

In our preferred specification, we define Z_j as the annual growth rate of real wages below the 40th percentile in country j (USA, UK and Germany) and wages in the construction and manufacturing sector for Ireland, expressed in zloty (we check the robustness of our results to the use of one alternative definition for Z_j as explained below). We have chosen to use the growth rate of mean wages below the 40th percentile to measure the attractiveness of destination countries for Polish emigrants as these end up in the lower part of the wage distribution in host countries, especially in the first years after migration. We demonstrate this in Figure 5, where we plot the position of Polish immigrants in the wage distribution for Germany, the US and the UK:

for all three countries, Poles are found in the lower part of the distribution of natives. For Ireland, where we do not have microdata, but aggregate data by industry, the 2006 Irish Census shows that over half of the Polish male immigrants work in construction and manufacturing. Moreover, we calculate wages in zloty, which accounts for fluctuations in the exchange rate of the US dollar, the British Pound and the Euro *vis-a vis* the Polish currency. This will matter, as a large part of earnings is likely to be spent in Poland, either through re-allocation to the families in form of remittances, or through temporariness of migrations, where savings are later spent at home (see e.g. Djajic, 1989, Dustmann, 1997). As we show in Table 8, such exchange rate fluctuations have been sizeable over the years we consider, and contributed substantially to changes in the earnings differential of Polish workers in Poland and abroad, in terms of their purchasing power in Poland.

We then allow the effect of each Z_t^j to differ across different Polish regions r by interacting Z_t^j with regional dummies R_r, and define $Z_{rt}^j = Z_t^j \times R_r$. Finally, we account for the change in the relative role of economic shocks in different countries on migration decisions caused by the 2004 EU enlargement. We define two dummy variables EU_1 and EU_2 that identify, respectively, the period in which Poland was not member of the EU (until 2003 included) and the years after Poland joined the EU (2004 onwards). We then interact Z_{rt}^j with EU_p ($p = 1, 2$) and define $Z_{rpt}^j = Z_{rt}^j \times EU_p$.

We have therefore a vector **Z** of 120 instruments (4 destination countries x 16 regions x 2 time periods; normalisation requires that 8 of these variables are set to zero, one region for each country for the years before 2004 and after 2004). Our first stage regression is:

$$m_{rt} = \sum_{j \in (UK, US, Germany)} \sum_{r=1}^{R} \sum_{p=1}^{2} b_{jrp} Z_{rpt}^j + X_{rt} g + \sum_{r=1}^{R} d_r R_r + \sum_{t=1}^{T} f_t \tau_t + v_{rt}$$

Each coefficient b_{jrp} captures the effect that a shock to destination country j has on the emigration rate in region r before ($p = 1$) or after ($p = 2$) Poland joining the EU, net of time-invariant region characteristics R_r, of nationwide time-varying shocks τ_t, and of other exogenous factors X_{rt}. We expect shocks to country j to have a higher impact on emigration (i.e. b_{jrp} to be larger) in regions where a larger fraction of total emigration is directed to that destination country. In figures 6 and 7 we plot for years before (figure 6) and after (figure 7) 2004 the estimated coefficients b_{jrp} versus the fraction of the mean number of emigrants over the mean population in period p from each region r in each destination country j. The figures show that the coefficients that weigh shocks in each country to different regions are positively correlated with the regional fraction of emigrants to that destination country, with the exception of the US and Ireland[21] for years before 2004. This reassures us that our coefficients b_{jrp} are picking up actual effects of destination country shocks on regional emigration.

One concern with this strategy is that the estimated weights b_{jrp} may not be entirely exogenous to region specific shocks, as the differential reactions of regional emigration to pull factors from destination countries may be due to potentially endogenous regional characteristics. Notice however that the estimated weights are only allowed to vary across destination-country pairs, for the period before and after the EU enlargement, and are otherwise time-invariant. Further, we include region fixed effects in our empirical model, which absorb all time invariant regional characteristics.

Nevertheless, as a robustness check we also provide IV estimates where we rely on preassigned regional weights (ω_r^j) to model the differential effects of destination countries' shocks on Polish regions, and use as instruments $\omega_r^j \times Z_t^j \times EU_p$. This reduces the dimensionality of our vector of instruments $\mathbf{Z}$ to 8. We experiment with two alternative weights ω_r^j.

First, we use as regional weights the inverse of the distance between each region's capital and the capital of the country of destination j. The assumption in this case is that migration costs increase with distance, and therefore destination countries' shocks have a higher pull effect on regions that are closer. Second, a number of papers have illustrated the importance of migration networks on migration decisions (see e.g. Munshi 2003 and Bartel 1989). We therefore expect shocks from country j to have a stronger pull effect on emigration from regions where a higher share of emigrants has settled previously. We do not have reliable data on historical regional emigration to different destination countries, so we cannot measure the historical strength of regional migration networks. However, we can measure the strength of regional migration networks to destination country j by using the mean share of emigrants from region r to country j over the years 1998-2007, where we exclude in every year t the share of emigrants in year $t-1$, t, and $t+1$ to reduce possible feedback in the construction of this variable. In practice, this means that we define for every year t_0 weights $\omega_{rt_0}^j$:

$$\omega_{rt_0}^j = \frac{1}{N_{t_0}} \sum_{t<t_0-1, t>t_0+1} emigrants_{rt}^j / emigrants_{rt}$$

where N_{r0} is the number of years over which the mean is computed in year t_0.

---

21 Notice however that the share of Polish emigrants in Ireland before 2004 is extremely low, and migration to the US has sharply declined over the period.

Finally, we check the robustness of our results to the use of alternative variables as "pull factors" Z_t^j. As we explain above, in our baseline results we define Z_t^j as the growth rate of average wages below the 40th percentile, expressed in zloty, in destination country j. We experiment with one alternative. We use as an alternative "pull factor" in year t for country j the deviation of the country's per capita GDP growth (see for instance McKenzie, Theoharides and Yang (2010) for evidence on the role of GDP growth in destination countries on migration choices), GDP_t^j, from the OECD mean[22], GDP_t^{OECD}. The variable $\Delta gdp_t^j = GDP_t^j - GDP_t^j$ captures the relative economic performance of country j relative to other OECD countries and hence we expect it to measure its relative attractiveness for potential migrants.

4. Results

4.1 Main findings

We report our baseline results in Table 9. Columns 1 and 2 in panel A report OLS estimates of β in expression (5), for average wages (row 1), and for wages of different education groups (rows 2 to 4). Column 1 reports results from a specification where we only control for regional fixed effects and year dummies, while column 2 reports results where we add controls for the size of the regional population, the average age in the region, and education and gender composition (see Section 3.2 for more details). All regressions refer to the years between 1998 and 2007. The estimates in row 1 show that emigration is associated with a higher growth of regional average wages: the estimated coefficient ranges between 0.97 in column 1 and 1 in column 2, and is in both cases statistically significant at the 10% level. As we explain in section 3, our OLS estimates are likely to be lower bound for the effect of emigration on regional wages.

In columns 3 and 4 in panel B we report IV estimates of the same coefficient, where we use as instruments wage growth (in Polish purchasing power) below the 40th percentile in each destination country, interacted with regional dummies, and with dummies for the period before and after EU accession, as we explain in section 3.4. We show first-stage statistics for our instruments in rows 5 (partial R-squared) and 6 (F-statistics for joint significance of excluded instruments) of Table 9. The partial R-squared is high, suggesting that our set of instruments explains about 90 percent of the variation in emigration rates. The F-statistics for significance of excluded instruments is 12.3 in the basic model (column 3) and 10.2 in the model with all controls (column 4), which is above the conventional threshold level of 10 and around the threshold suggested by Stock and Yogo

---

22 The GDP is in both cases in US constant dollars. Source: OECD.Stat Extracts (http://stats.oecd.org/Index.aspx).

(2005) for a large set of instruments.[23] IV estimates are very close to the OLS estimates, pointing at emigration having a positive effect on average wages in Poland. These are short-run estimates, as the variation we use for estimation is the change in the stock of emigrants between years. As we show in our theoretical discussion of section 3.1, a positive overall effect of emigration is compatible with the elasticity of capital supply not being infinite, at least in the short run. In terms of magnitude, the estimates in columns 2 and 4 imply that an increase of one percentage point in the ratio of emigrants to the total population led to a 0.97%-1.01% increase in average real wages. Over the period we consider, emigration from Poland increased on average by 0.19 percentage points per year, and real wages increased by about 1.7% per year. Thus, these estimates suggest that emigration contributed about 11% to overall wage growth.

In Rows 2-4 of Table 9, we report results for the three different education groups. The figures in Table 3 show that emigration was mainly concentrated in the middle part of the educational distribution, and far less at the bottom. According to the model we develop in Section 3, the effect of emigration should therefore be felt particularly for the intermediately educated, as this group experienced the largest (negative) relative supply shock. Results in rows 2-4 of Table 9 are in line with these predictions, suggesting that emigration led to an increase in wages for medium-and highly educated workers, but possibly depressed wages for low educated workers. The average annual growth rate of wages between 1998 and 2007 was 1.3% for low educated workers, 1.4% for the intermediate education group, and 1.2% for the highly educated. Thus, our point estimates in columns 3 and 4 imply that emigration kept reduced wage growth for low educated workers by between 17% and 31%, while it contributed positively to wage growth for the intermediate education group (by about 18%), and for highly educated workers (by between 18% and 24%). Estimates for the low educated are however not significantly different from zero.

Overall, these results are remarkably in line with the predictions of the simple model we show in section 3, with larger gains for workers in skill categories that were exposed to a larger negative supply shock. They also indicate that emigration helped overall wage growth in Poland over the period, possibly reducing however the returns to capital, which became – through a reduction in labour supply – relatively more abundant.

---

23 According to the tabulations of Stock and Yogo (2005) the critical value for the F-statistics when using 120 instruments is 11.31.

4.2 Additional Results and Robustness Checks

We now provide additional results and robustness checks to account for the data limitations we have outlined in section 2.3, and to address possible problems with our IV strategy, as discussed in section 3.4.

In Table 10 we present OLS and IV results from specifications with all controls (equivalent to those in columns 2 and 4 of Table 9) where we account for the potential limitations in our data. In panel A, we use gross wages as dependent variable, which we have constructed from the net wage information and information on individual characteristics (see Appendix A.3 for details). Results are very similar to those we present in Table 9, with the estimates for the low educated being slightly larger, but not significantly different from zero. In panel B, we account for non-response to the wage question in the PLFS by imputing wages for those individuals who report missing wage information (see Appendix A4 for details about wage imputation). Estimates are in line with our baseline results in Table 9, although the estimated coefficients are slightly smaller in magnitude.

In panel C, we report results where we correct the measurement of the emigration share for possible undercounting due to single emigrant households which we do not capture in our data. We assume that single households are as frequent among emigrants as among non-emigrants, within the same age-education group in every region and year, and we rescale the number of emigrants accordingly (see Appendix A.5 for details). This slightly reduces the size of all estimated coefficients relative to the baseline, with the exception of low educated workers, which is now slightly larger. Finally, in panel D, we use a measure of average regional wages which is adjusted for possible composition effects. We adopt a two step procedure: first, for each year we estimate individual log wage regressions controlling for age, gender and education. We then take the average regional log-wage residuals, or the average regional log-wage residuals by education group, as dependent variable. Results are again similar, although the estimated effect on wages of primary educated individuals is smaller than in previous estimates.

In Table 11 we report results obtained with different instrumental variables (see section 3.4 for details), where in each panel, results in column (1) refer to specifications without any controls except for region and year dummies, and results in column (2) to specifications where we include all control variables. In Panel A we use as instruments the deviation in each of the destination countries' GDP per capita growth rate relative to the OECD mean, interacted with regional dummies and EU accession dummies. The first stage statistics, reported in rows 5 and 6, indicate that these instruments are weaker than our preferred instruments based on wage growth in the bottom part of the wage distribution of destination countries. Nevertheless, results with both sets of instruments are very similar.

In Panel B and C we present IV estimates where we have reduced the dimensionality of our instruments. In Panel B we use the inverse of the distance between each region and the destination country to weight destination countries' growth of wages below the 40th percentile. Panel C, instead, uses destination countries' wage growth, but weighted with the mean (over time) of the regional emigration share to each destination country. The Partial R-squared (F-statistics) are lower in both cases, ranging between 0.13 (2.06) in Panel B and 0.24 (4.43) in Panel C. Estimates in Panel B and C are qualitatively similar to tour baseline IV results, despite coming from weaker instruments. Overall, the IV results are remarkably stable despite the different instruments and weights that we are using, and confirm the pattern of the OLS results, suggesting that workers in the intermediate skill category, which experienced the largest negative supply shock, have gained most in terms of wages.

Overall, our findings suggest that emigration from Poland over the period between 1998 and 2007 has had a slightly positive (although not always precisely estimated) effect on average wages of those who did not emigrate. Within our theoretical framework (see section 2), this implies that the supply of capital was – at least in the short run – not perfectly elastic. Further, the impact migration had on wages for the different skill groups seems to mirror the relative negative supply shocks experienced by these skill groups through emigration: Emigrants were mainly drawn from the medium and upper parts of the educational distribution, and it is here where we find the more pronounced positive wage effects. On the other hand, there was far less emigration by those in the lowest educational category, and the negative estimates we obtain are compatible with this.

5. Discussion and Conclusions

We use the Polish Labour Force Survey to assess the effect that emigration over the period between 1998 and 2007 – a period of large out-migration – had on the wages of Polish workers who did not emigrate. The PLFS is unique in that it asks households about household members who have migrated, which allows direct measurement of the migrant population. In addition, the survey provides information about key characteristics of emigrants, like their age and education. We use this data to construct region-and skill group specific emigration rates.

Our basic results suggest that the large emigration Poland has experienced over the period between 1998 and 2007 (with the share of emigrants increasing from 0.5 to 2.3 percent, and in some regions up to 5.6 percent) contributed to overall wage growth. This is particularly so for workers in the intermediate skill group, which experienced the largest negative labour supply shock. Our basic specification regresses variation in skill group specific wage rates on region specific emigration rates, conditioning on the age and education composition and on region fixed effects. While these fixed effects estimates are potentially biased, as emigration may be larger in regions that experienced negative shocks, the bias is likely to be downwards, which allows us to interpret our results as lower bounds. To investigate this further, we implement an IV strategy. The information in the PLFS to what country emigrants have migrated allows us construct an instrument, based on labour market shocks to the various destination countries. Our basic IV results are very similar to the fixed effect results, and reconfirm a slight overall positive effect of emigration, with individuals in the intermediate education group gaining most. These results are robust to various checks on the definition of the wage variables, where we account for missing information and for the effects of the fiscal system, and on the potential mismeasurement of regional emigration rates. We provide also estimates using different IV strategies, with similar results.

All this suggests that emigration had a positive effect on Polish wages over the period we consider, in particular for workers in the intermediate skill group – which was also the group with the highest relative out-migration. However, not everyone gained: Our point estimates suggest that low educated workers – the group that emigrated least, and thus became relatively more abundant – did not experience wage gains, and may even have experienced slight wage decreases, although estimates are insignificant for this skill group in most cases. Further, the overall positive wage effect we find point at capital being inelastic in supply at least in the short run. Therefore, although Polish outmigration is likely to have led to positive wages effects on average, not all workers have gained. Furthermore, the negative supply shock that was relatively more pronounced for intermediate and highly educated workers may have had negative consequences for the Polish economy during a period where skilled labour was likely to be important. Our analysis has nothing to say about these effects, but our results call for future work that investigates the overall effects of outmigration on the Polish economy.

References

Altonji, Joseph G., and David Card. 1991. "The Effects of Immigration on the Labor Market Outcomes of Less-Skilled Natives." In *John M. Abowd and Richard B. Freeman, (eds.), Immigration, trade and the labor market*, University Chicago Press, , p. 201-234.

Angrist, Joshua D., and Adriane D. Kugler. 2003. "Protective or Counter-Productive? Labour Market Institutions and the Effect of Immigration on EU Natives." *Economic Journal* 113(488): F302-F331.

Angrist, Joshua D., and Jörn-Steffen Pischke. *Mostly Harmless Econometrics: An Empiricist's Companion*. Princeton University Press.

Aydemir, Abdurrahman, and George J. Borjas. 2007. "Cross-Country Variation in the Impact of International Migration: Canada, Mexico, and the United States." *Journal of the European Economic Association* 5(4): 663-708.

Bartel, Ann. 1989. "Where Do the New U.S. Immigrants Live?" *Journal of Labor Economics* 7(4): 371-91.

Bianchi, Milo, Paolo Buonanno, and Paolo Pinotti. 2011. "Do Immigrants Cause Crime?" *Journal of the European Economic Association, forthcoming*.

Borjas, George J. 2003. "The Labor Demand Curve Is Downward Sloping: Reexamining The Impact Of Immigration On The Labor Market." *The Quarterly Journal of Economics* 118(4): 1335-1374.

Borjas, George J., Richard B. Freeman, and Lawrence F. Katz. 1997. "How Much Do Immigration and Trade Affect Labor Market Outcomes?" *Brookings Papers on Economic Activity* 1997(1): 1-90.

——. 1996. "Searching for the Effect of Immigration on the Labor Market." *American Economic Review* 86(2): 246-251.

Card, David. 2001. "Immigrant Inflows, Native Outflows and the Local Labor Market Impacts of Immigration." *Journal of Labor Economics* 19(1): 22-64.

Card, David, and John DiNardo. 2000. "Do Immigrant Inflows Lead to Native Outflows?" *The American Economic Review, Papers and Proceedings of the One Hundred Twelfth Annual Meeting of the American Economic Association* 90(2): 360-367.

Card, David, and Ethan G. Lewis. 2007. "The Diffusion of Mexican Immigrants During the 1990s: Explanations and Impacts." In *George J. Borjas (editor), Mexican Immigration*, Chicago: University of Chicago Press (for NBER).

Cortes, Patricia. 2008. "The Effect of Low-Skilled Immigration on U.S. Prices: Evidence from CPI Data." *Journal of Political Economy* 116(3): 381-422.

D'Amuri, Francesco, Gianmarco I. P. Ottaviano, and Giovanni Peri. 2010. "The Labor Market Impact of Immigration in Western Germany in the 1990s." *European Economic Review* 54(4): 550-570.

Djajic, Slobodan. 1989. "Migrants in a guest-worker system: A utility maximizing approach." *Journal of Development Economics* 31(2): 327-339.

Docquier, Frédéric, Çaglar 'Ozden, and Giovanni Peri. 2011. "The Labor Market Effects of Immigration and Emigration in OECD Countries." *IZA DP No. 6258*.

Dustmann, Christian. 1997. "Return Migration, Uncertainty and Precautionary Savings." *Journal of Development Economics,* 52(2): 295-316.

Dustmann, Christian, and Albrecht Glitz. 2011. "'How Do Industries and Firms Respond to Changes in Local Labor Supply?'" *CReAM DP 18/11*.

Dustmann, Christian, Francesca Fabbri, and Ian Preston. 2005. "The Impact of Immigration on the UK Labour Market." *Economic Journal* 115(507): F324-F341.

Dustmann, Christian, Tommaso Frattini, and Ian Preston. 2012. "The Effect of Immigration along the Distribution of Wages." *The Review of Economics Studies, forthcoming*.

Elsner, Benjamin. 2010. "Does Emigration Benefit the Stayers? The EU Enlargement as a Natural Experiment. Evidence from Lithuania." *FEEM Nota di Lavoro* 151.

———. 2011. "Emigration and Wages: The EU Enlargement Experiment." *IZA DP No. 6111*.

Fassmann, Heinz, and Rainer Munz. 1994. "European East-West Migration, 1945-1992." *International Migration Review* 28(3): 520-538.

Fiorio, Carlo V. 2004. "Confidence intervals for kernel density estimation." *The Stata Journal* 4(2): 103-114.

Frattini, Tommaso. 2010. "Immigration and Prices in the UK." *Manuscript, University of Milan*.

Gandal, Neil, Gordon H. Hanson, and Matthew J. Slaughter. 2004. "Technology, Trade, and Adjustment to Immigration in Israel." *European Economic Review* 48(2): 403-428.

Glitz, Albrecht. 2012. "The Labor Market Impact of Immigration: A Quasi-Experiment Exploiting Immigrant Location Rules in Germany." *Journal of Labor Economics* 30(1): 175-213.

Gonzalez, Libertad, and Francesc Ortega. 2011. "How Do Very Open Economies Absorb Large Immigration Flows? Evidence from Spanish Regions." *Labour Economics* 18(1): 57-70.

Hall, Peter. "Effect of bias estimation on coverage accuracy of bootstrap confidence intervals for a probability density." *Annals of Statistics* 20(2): 675-694.

Hanson, Gordon. 2007. "Emigration, Labor Supply and Earnings in Mexico." In *George J. Borjas (editor), Mexican Immigration*, Chicago: University of Chicago Press (for NBER), p. 289-328.

Hanson, Gordon H., and Matthew J. Slaughter. 2002. "Labor-Market Adjustment in Open Economies: Evidence from US States." *Journal of International Economics* 57(1): 3-29.

Home Office, UK Border Agency. 2009. "Accession Monitoring Report, May 2004 December 2008, A8 Countries."

Horowitz, Joel L. "The bootstrap." In *Handbook of Econometrics, ed. J. J. Heckman and E. Leamer*, , p. 3159–3228.

Irish Central Stastical Office. 2008. "Census 2006 Non-Irish Nationals Living in Ireland. Profiles of Nationalities -UK, Polish, Lithuanian, Nigerian, Latvian."

Jaeger, David A. "'Skill Differences and the Effect of Immigrants on the Wages of Natives'." *mimeo, College of William and Mary*.

Kaczmarczyk, Paweł, and Marek Okólski. 2008. "Demographic and Labou- Market Impacts of Migration on Poland." *Oxford Review Economic Policy* 24(3): 599-624.

Kaczmarczyk, Paweł, Marta Mioduszewska, and Anna Zylicz. 2009. "Impact of the Post-Accession Migration on the Polish Labour Market." In *Kahanec, Martin, & Zimmermann, Klaus F. (eds.), EU Enlargement and the Labor Markets: What Do We Know?*, Springer-Verlag Berlin, p. 219-253.

Kupiszewski, Marek (editor). 2007. "Long-term international migration scenarios for Europe, 2002-2052." *CEFMR Working Paper 3/2007*.

Lewis, Ethan G. 2011. "Immigration, Skill Mix, and Capital-Skill Complementarity." *The Quarterly Journal of Economics* 126(2): 1029-1069.

——. 2003. "Local, Open Economies Within the US: How Do Industries Respond to Immigration?" *Federal Reserve Bank of Philadelphia* WP 04-01.

Manacorda, Marco, Alan Manning, and Jonathan Wadsworth. 2012. "The Impact of Immigration on the Structure of Wages: Theory and Evidence from Britain." *Journal of the European Economic Association* 10(1): 120-151.

Mckenzie, David, Caroline Theoharides, and Dean Yang. 2010. "How Important are Destination Country Macro Shocks in Determining Migration Flows? Evidence from Filipino Migration." *Manuscript, University of Michigan*.

Ministry of Economy and Labour. 2005. "Employment in Poland."

Mishra, Prachi. 2007. "Emigration and Wages in Source Countries: Evidence from Mexico." *Journal of Development Economics* 82(1): 180-199.

Mostwin, Danuta. 1969. "Post-World War II Polish Immigrants in the United States." *Polish American Studies* 26(2): 5-14.

Munshi, Kaivan. 2003. "Networks in the Modern Economy: Mexican Migrants in the U.S. Labor Market." *The Quarterly Journal of Economics* 118(3): 549-599.

Newey, Whitney K., and Kenneth D. West. 1994. "Automatic Lag Selection in Covariance Matrix Estimation." *The Review of Economic Studies* 61(4): 631-653.

Ottaviano, Gianmarco I. P., and Giovanni Peri. 2012. "Rethinking the Effects of Immigration on Wages." *Journal of the European Economic Association* 10(1): 152-197.

Quispe-Agnoli, Myriam, and Madeline Zavodny. 2002. "The Effect of Immigration on Output Mix, Capital, and Productivity." *FRB Atlanta Economic Review* (1): 17-27.

Staiger, Douglas, and James H. Stock. 1997. "Instrumental Variables Regression with Weak Instruments." *Econometrica* 65(3): 557-586.

Stock, James H., and Motohiro Yogo. 2005. "Testing for Weak Instruments in Linear IV Regression." In *Donald W.K. Andrews (editor), Identification and Inference for Econometric Models.*, New York: Cambridge University Press, p. 80-108.

Zubrzycki, Jerzy. 1953. "Emigration from Poland in the Nineteenth and Twentieth Centuries." *Population Studies* 6(3): 248-272.

A Data Appendix

A.1 Sample extraction

Poland is divided into 16 regions: Greater Poland (*województwo* wielkopolskie), Kuyavian-Pomeranian (*województwo kujawsko-pomorskie*), Lesser Poland (*województwo małopolskie*), Łódź Voivodeship (*województwo łódzkie*), Lower Silesian (*województwo dolnośląskie*), Lublin (*województwo lubelskie*), Lubusz (*województwo lubuskie*), Masovian (*województwo mazowieckie*), Opole (*województwo opolskie*), Podlaskie (*województwo podlaskie*), Pomeranian (*województwo pomorskie*), Silesian (*województwo śląskie*), Subcarpathian (*województwo podkarpackie*), Świętokrzyskie (*województwo świętokrzyskie*), Warmian-Masurian (*województwo warmińsko-mazurskie*), West Pomeranian (*województwo zachodniopomorskie*). In our analysis, each region is considered as a separate labour market. The average regional labour force (active and inactive) is about 1.7milion, where the biggest region in both 1998 and 2007 is Masovian, the region of Warsaw; the smallest region is Lubusz in 1998, and Opole in 2007. In Figure A1 and A2, we show a map of Poland with the 16 provinces and, respectively, the yearly average wage increase and the yearly average change in the share of emigrants between 1998 and 2007.

For our analysis we use data from 1998 to 2007. We restrict the sample to those who are between 15 and 65 years old. We eliminate wage observations below the 1st percentile and above the 99th percentile to eliminate outliers. To avoid selection problems due to the change in the composition of the sample, we compute regional average wages by year, and we drop all individuals from the sample who are either return migrants, or emigrate within the next year, to keep the sample we use to compute the regional average wages constant. Mean wages by region are calculated using population weights provided in the survey.

The variable *education* is defined by recoding the original variable in the survey (which was classified in nine categories) into three categories. We define as *low educated* all those individuals who have partially of fully completed primary school, or equivalently have 8 or less years of education ("*bez wykształcenia szkolnego*", "*niepełne podstawowe*" and "*podstawowe*"), *intermediately educated* all those individuals who have completed a vocational or general secondary education, and have between 9 and 13 years of education ("*średnie zawodowe*", "*średnie ogólnokształcące*", "*gimnazjum*"and "*zasadnicze zawodowe*"), and as *highly educated* all those who have a post-secondary or higher education, or more than 13 years of schooling ("*wyższe*", and"*policealne*").

A.2 The weights: estimation strategy

In the dataset for emigrants, no sampling weights are reported. As we explain in the main text, we therefore estimate the weights for emigrants based on the weights we have for those who are in the labour force. Using the information provided by the Polish Statistical Office, we know that the sampling units are households and the first strata of the sampling procedure are regions. Weights are then defined on the basis of the response rate and some other demographic variables (place of residence, gender and age). Based on this information, we estimate the following regression for each year t, quarter q, and gender s:

$$weights_{itqs} = \sum_{r=1}^{R}\sum_{d=1}^{D}\sum_{y=1900}^{Y} \beta_{rdytqs} R_r * D_{itqs} * Y_{itqs} + u_{itqs} \text{ for } \forall t,q,s$$

where R are regional dummies, D_{itqs} are eight dummies for the size of the town where the household resides, Y_{itqs} are year-of-birth dummies, and u_{itqs} is an error term. We use the regression to estimate the weights for emigrants[24]. These weights are used to compute most of the information for emigrants, like total number of emigrants and the share of emigrants in the total population.

A.3 Net and gross wages

The Polish LFS contains information about net monthly wages. There are three tax rates in Poland[25], which identify two tax base thresholds. We apply the following formula:

$$grosswages_{it} = \begin{cases} \dfrac{netwages_{it} - TC_t}{1-\tau_t^L} & \text{if } netwages_{it} \leq x_t^{L,N} \\[2ex] \dfrac{netwages_{it} - TC_t + x_t^{L,G}(\tau_t^L - \tau_t^M)}{1-\tau_t^M} & \text{if } x_t^{L,N} < netwages_{it} \leq x_t^{H,N} \\[2ex] \dfrac{netwages_{it} - TC_t + x_t^{L,G}(\tau_t^L - \tau_t^M) + x_t^{H,G}(\tau_t^M - \tau_t^H)}{1-\tau_t^H} & \text{if } netwages_{it} > x_t^{H,N} \end{cases}$$

Where $grosswages_{it}$ are the yearly gross wages for individual i at time t; $netwages_{it}$ are yearly net wages; TC_t are the tax credits individuals are eligible to; x_t are the tax base thresholds, where b = L(low), H(high), and j = N(net), G(gross). We

---

24 For emigrants, there is no information on the size of town of residence before they moved abroad. However, we have information on the household the emigrant belonged to before emigrating. Based on that we assign the size of the town to the emigrant.

25 Poland has an individual taxation system, but taxpayers can decide to pool their income with the income of other people in the family. Since we do not observe the actual behaviour of households, we compute gross wages under the assumption that workers do not choose to pool earnings.

apply the net threshold to our data ($x_t^{L,N} = x_t^{L,G}(1-\tau_t^L)$; $x_t^{H,N} = x_t^{H,G}(1-\tau_t^M)$). The fiscal year in Poland corresponds to the calendar year. For each individual, we compute the yearly net wage (from the monthly net wages reported in the survey) and assign individuals to the respective tax base bracket.

In 1999, a tax reform introduced the obligation for employees to pay their own social contributions, which, before 1999, were paid by the employers. In order to make gross wages comparable across years[26], we compute gross wages net of employees' social contributions. Finally, we divide the yearly gross wages by twelve in order to obtain monthly gross wages to use in the econometric analysis.

A.4 Missing wages

Non-response rate to the wage question in the Polish Labour Force Survey has increased in the later years, from 17% in 1998 to 32% in 2007. Moreover, non-responses are overrepresented among the better educated. This may lead to under- or over-estimating the effect of emigration, depending on the type of selection. To check robustness of our results, we correct for differential non response rates across different population groups, and impute wages for those employed individuals that have missing wage information. Under the assumption that the probability of response to the wage question depends only on observable characteristics, this procedure allows recovering measures of regional average log wages. Our imputation procedure works as follows. First, we run separately for each year, quarter and gender, regressions of log-wages controlling for age, education and their interaction, occupation, marital status, part-time work, whether the individual is a public sector employee, city size and region of residence.[28] We use the estimated coefficients to predict wages for all employees in the sample for whom wage information is missing. We add an error term to the prediction, drawn from a normal distribution, with zero mean and heteroskedastic variance according to age, education and gender. We use these wages to compute regional means to be used in the econometric analysis.

A.5 Emigrant share

We do not observe emigrants who live in single households before emigration, which implies that we may be underestimating the number of Polish emigrants. As we explain in Section 2.3, we do not believe that this is a serious problem, given the low percentage of single household in the age range where most

---

26 We control for age using dummies for 10 years age brackets. Education is expressed with dummies for low, intermediate and high education. Occupation controls are dummies for each 1-digit ISCO08 occupation group. Controls for city size are dummy variables for seven size categories. Region of residence is controlled with dummies for each *voivodship*.

migrations take place, and we demonstrate that our data on emigration to different countries closely resembles those we construct from data sources in the receiving countries. Despite that, we provide also estimates where we reconstruct the share of single household emigrants, using information on the share of single households among non-emigrants.

To accomplish that, we first compute the share of individuals living in a single household in the resident population in year t, region r, age group a (we use five 10-year age brackets) and education level e (we use three education levels), α_{raet}. Under the assumption that the share of single households, conditional on observable characteristics, is the same among residents and emigrants, we can then rescale the number of observed emigrants in each year-region-ageeducation cell E^*_{raet} by $1/1 - \alpha_{raet}$ to obtain an estimate on the actual number of emigrants in that cell, $E_{raet} = E^*_{raet}/1 - \alpha_{raet}$. We then sum up the adjusted numbers of emigrants by region and year and we compute the shares to be used in the regression. Adjusting for undercounting of single households, the share of emigrants in the total working age pupulation is 0.7% in 1998 and 2.8% in 2007, which compares with 0.5% and 2.3%, respectively, without the adjustment.

B The Theoretical Model

B.1 Wage Determination: CES Production

In the derivations below, we closely follow Dustmann, Frattini and Preston (2012). Suppose production of a single good y uses combines capital K and labour H, using a CES nested production function:

$$y = \left[\beta H^s + (1-\beta)K^s\right]^{1/s}$$

Labour H is a CES composite, which consists of different labour types i:

$$H = \left[\sum_i \alpha_i l_i^\sigma\right]^{1/\sigma} \tag{B.1.a}$$

Where, in the production function, $s \leq 1$ is the elasticity of substitution between capital and labour, β is the relative productivity of labour and capital. In the labour function, α_i determines productivity of the *ith* type of labour and $\sigma \leq 1$ determines the elasticity of substitution between labour types.

In order to obtain the equilibrium values for the wages (w_i) and the return to capital (ρ), we compute the first order conditions of the production function with respect to the labour type i (equation B.1.b) and capital (equation B.1.c), respectively.

$$w_i = \frac{\partial y}{\partial l_i} = \beta \alpha_i \left[\beta H^s + (1-\beta)K^s\right]^{\frac{1}{s}-1} * H^{s-\sigma} l_i^{\sigma-1}$$

$$\ln w_i = \ln \frac{\partial y}{\partial l_i} = \ln \beta \alpha_i + \left(\frac{1}{s}-1\right)\ln H^s\left[\beta + (1-\beta)\frac{K^s}{H^s}\right] + (s-\sigma)\ln H + (\sigma-1)\ln l_i$$

$$= \ln \beta \alpha_i + \frac{(1-\sigma)}{\sigma}\ln\left[\sum_j \alpha_j(\pi_j^0 - \pi_j^1 m)^\sigma\right] + (\sigma-1)\ln(\pi_i^0 - \pi_i^1 m) + \left(\frac{1}{s}-1\right)\ln\left[\beta + (1-\beta)\frac{K^s}{H^s}\right] \tag{B.1.b}$$

$$\rho = \frac{\partial y}{\partial K} = (1-\beta)\left[\beta H^s + (1-\beta)\left(\frac{K}{H}\right)^s\right]^{\frac{1}{s}-1} K^{s-1}$$

$$\ln \rho = \ln \frac{\partial y}{\partial K}$$

$$= \ln(1-\beta) + \left(\frac{1}{s} - 1\right)\ln\left[\beta H^s + (1-\beta)\left(\frac{K}{H}\right)^s\right] + (s-1)\ln K$$

$$= \ln(1-\beta) + (s-1)\ln\left(\frac{K}{H}\right) + \left(\frac{1}{s} - 1\right)\ln\left[\beta + (1-\beta)\left(\frac{K}{H}\right)^s\right] \qquad \text{(B.1.c)}$$

B.2 First order effect of emigration on the wage distribution

$$\frac{d\ln w_i}{dm} = (1-\sigma)\left(-\sum_i \frac{\alpha_i \pi_i^1 (\pi_i^0 - \pi_i^1 m)^{\sigma-1}}{\sum_j \alpha_j (\pi_j^0 - \pi_j^1 m)^\sigma}\right) + (1-\sigma)\frac{\pi_i^1}{\pi_i^0 - \pi_i^1 m} + (1-s)(1-\psi)\left(\frac{d\ln K}{dm} - \frac{d\ln H}{dm}\right)$$

$$= (1-\sigma)\frac{d\ln H}{dm} + (1-\sigma)\frac{\pi_i^1}{\pi_i^0 - \pi_i^1 m} + (1-s)(1-\psi)\left(\frac{d\ln K}{dm} - \frac{d\ln H}{dm}\right)$$

$$\frac{d\ln H}{dm} = \left(-\sum_i \frac{\alpha_i \pi_i^1 (\pi_i^0 - \pi_i^1 m)^{\sigma-1}}{\sum_j \alpha_j (\pi_j^0 - \pi_j^1 m)^\sigma}\right) = -\sum_i \omega_i \frac{\pi_i^1}{\pi_i^0 - \pi_i^1 m}$$

$$\frac{d\ln \rho}{dk} = -(1-s)\psi\left[\frac{d\ln K}{dm} - \frac{d\ln H}{dm}\right]$$

Where $\omega_i = \dfrac{\alpha_i (\pi_i^0)^\sigma}{\sum_j \alpha_j (\pi_j^0)^\sigma}$ is the share of the ith type in the labour aggregate H^σ and

$\psi = \dfrac{\beta H^s}{\beta H^s + (1-\beta)K^s}$ is the share of labour in the CES aggregate y^s

The elasticity of supply of capital is $\theta = \dfrac{d\ln K}{d\ln \rho}$, where $\dfrac{d\ln K}{dm} = \theta\dfrac{d\ln \rho}{dm}$ and we

substitute this into the expression for $\dfrac{d\ln \rho}{dm}$ we obtain:

$$\frac{d\ln\rho}{dm} = -(1-s)\psi\left(\theta\frac{d\ln\rho}{dm} - \frac{d\ln H}{dm}\right)$$

$$= \frac{(1-s)\psi}{1+(1-s)\psi\theta}\frac{d\ln H}{dm}$$

And thus

$$\frac{d\ln w_i}{dm} = (1-\sigma)\frac{d\ln H}{dm} + (1-\sigma)\frac{\pi_i^1}{\pi_i^0 - \pi_i^1 m} + (1-s)(1-\psi)\left(\theta\frac{d\ln\rho}{dm} - \frac{d\ln H}{dm}\right)$$

$$= (1-\sigma)\frac{d\ln H}{dm} + (1-\sigma)\frac{\pi_i^1}{\pi_i^0 - \pi_i^1 m} - \frac{(1-s)(1-\psi)}{(1-s)\psi}\frac{d\ln\rho}{dm}$$

$$= (1-\sigma)\frac{d\ln H}{dm} + (1-\sigma)\frac{\pi_i^1}{\pi_i^0 - \pi_i^1 m} - \frac{(1-\psi)}{\psi}\frac{d\ln\rho}{dm}$$

$$= (1-\sigma)\frac{d\ln H}{dm} + (1-\sigma)\frac{\pi_i^1}{\pi_i^0 - \pi_i^1 m} - \frac{(1-\psi)}{\psi}\left(\frac{(1-s)\psi}{1+(1-s)\psi\theta}\frac{d\ln H}{dm}\right)$$

$$= (1-\sigma)\left\{\frac{\pi_i^1}{\pi_i^0 - \pi_i^1 m} - \phi\sum_j \omega_j \frac{\pi_j^1}{\pi_j^0 - \pi_j^1 m}\right\} \quad (B.1.d)$$

We define as $\phi = 1 + \frac{(1-s)(1-\psi)}{1+(1-s)\psi\theta}\frac{1}{(\sigma-1)} \leq 1$; $\phi = 1$ when we have perfectly elastic supply of capital ($\theta = \infty$), perfect substitutability of capital and labour ($s = 1$) or capital share is zero ($\psi = 1$).

If we set $m = 0$ then we get:

$$\left.\frac{d\ln w_i}{dm}\right|_{m=0} = (1-\sigma)\left\{\frac{\pi_i^1}{\pi_i^0} - \phi\sum_j \omega_j \frac{\pi_j^1}{\pi_j^0}\right\} \quad (B.1.e)$$

B.3 First order effect of emigration on the mean wages of the total population

At $m = 0$, $w_i \pi_i = \omega_i \bar{w}^0$ where $\bar{w}$ denotes the mean wage at $m = 0$. Hence the first order effect of emigration of mean wages in the pre-existing population is

$$\left.\frac{d \sum w_i \pi_i^0}{dm}\right|_{m=0} = \sum \pi_i^0 w_i \left.\frac{d \ln w_i}{dm}\right|_{m=0} = \sum \omega_i \bar{w}^0 \left.\frac{d \ln w_i}{dm}\right|_{m=0} = \sum \omega_i \bar{w}^0 (1-\sigma) \left\{ \frac{\pi_i^1}{\pi_i^0} - \phi \sum_j \omega_j \frac{\pi_j^1}{\pi_j^0} \right\} =$$

$$= (1-\sigma)(1-\phi)\bar{w}^0 \sum_i \omega_i \frac{\pi_i^1}{\pi_i^0} \geq 0$$

This is nonnegative as $\sigma \leq 1$ and $\phi \leq 1$

B.4 First order Taylor expansion around m=0

We use the expression $\left.\frac{d \ln w_i}{dm}\right|_{m=0} = (1-\sigma)\left\{\frac{\pi_i^1}{\pi_i^0} - \phi \sum_j \omega_j \frac{\pi_j^1}{\pi_j^0}\right\}$ in order to obtain a first order Taylor expansion around m=0 of the log wages expression (2) in the text.

$$\ln w_i = \ln \beta \alpha_i + \frac{(1-\sigma)}{\sigma} \ln \left[\sum_j \alpha_i (\pi_j^0)^\sigma\right] + (\sigma-1)\ln(\pi_i^0) + G(\rho_0) + (1-\sigma)\left\{\frac{\pi_i^1}{\pi_i^0} - \phi \sum_j \omega_j \frac{\pi_j^1}{\pi_j^0}\right\} m$$

Where: $G(\rho_0) = \ln\left(\frac{\rho}{1-\beta}\right) + (s-1)\ln\left(\frac{K}{H}\right)$

$$G(\rho_0) = \ln\left(\frac{\rho}{1-\beta}\right) + \frac{(s-1)}{s} \ln\left(\frac{1}{\beta}\left(\frac{\rho}{1-\beta}\right)^{\frac{s}{(1-s)}} - \frac{1-\beta}{\beta}\right)$$

We use the following model, as a consequence of the previous expansion:
$\ln w_{irt} = a_{ir} + b_{it} + c_i X_{rt} + \beta_i m_{rt} + \varepsilon_{irt}$

C The Polish Economy and the Polish labour market

The Polish economy has been growing rapidly over the last 15 years. Except for a period of lower growth between 2001 and 2002 due to the 1998 Russian crisis that affected also Poland, GDP growth was always above 3% (Figure C1), but decreased after 2008, due to the global financial crisis.[27] GDP growth was triggered mainly by capital formation, high consumption expenditure (both public and individual) and increasing exports and imports (Fihel et al., 2008).

As illustrated in Table 8, the Polish Zloty appreciated after 2004 in terms of some main currencies – dollar, pound and euro. Between 2004 and 2007, the Polish currency increased by almost 20% with respect to the euro and pound and by more than 20% with respect to the US dollar. Exchange rates together with price levels have often been considered determinants of the migration decision: they are important for saving and consumption preferences and for the choice of temporary or permanent migration (Djajic, 1989, Dustmann, 1997). When the zloty gained value, in particular after 2007, emigration from Poland decreased.

The last one and a half decades witnessed also a rapid improvement of most labour market indicators: unemployment decreased, wages increased, and the skill distribution of workers improved; further, there was a dramatic shift of the employment from the public to the private sector. In Figure C2, we plot the employment rate for the total population and for each education group. This graph shows the drop in employment in the early 2000s, and the rapid increase from 2002 onwards.[28] In the period between 1998 and 2002, the Polish labour market suffered as a consequence of the 1998 financial Russian crisis (also known as Rouble crisis, as the Russian currency collapsed)[29]. Employment by education and age groups exhibited similar trends, with the primary educated reaching the lowest level of employment in 2002 (24%) (see Figure C2).The participation

---

27 Poland has been less affected by the financial crisis compared to other EU countries. If we look at the data in 2008, other EU27 countries grew by 0.3%, whereas Poland was among the five European countries with the highest GDP growth rates, with a real growth rate of 5.1% with respect to 2007. The other countries were Romania, Montenegro, Bulgaria and Slovakia. More interesting, in 2009, Poland was the only country with a GDP growth rate of 1.6% across all EU27. This may explain why emigration decreased after 2008 (See Eurostat http://epp.eurostat.ec.europa.eu/tgm/table.do?tab=table&plugin=1&language=en&pcode=tsieb020).

28 The employment rate is defined as the number of employed over the working age population (16 to 64), while the unemployment rate is defined as the number of unemployed over the labour force (excluding inactive workers).

29 This crisis led to a demand shock that affected the Polish labour market according (see Ministry of Economyand Labour, Employment in Poland 2005.

rate[30] of workers has remained stable over the years. After 2002, the economy started to recover from the crisis, and both employment and wages increased again. Some observers think that while the economy was booming and new jobs were created, the country suffered from a shortage of labour, which could have hindered economic development. As reported in Kupiszewski (2007), this shortage created problems of mismatch between demand and supply for different skill groups, in particular for the high and medium skilled.

The above factors and the fast growing economy increased the pressure on wages (Figure C3), especially over more recent years. Between 2005 and 2007, wages increased by almost 10% (about 5% yearly). Mean wages increased before 2000 by about 2% yearly, but slightly decreased between 2000 and 2004, coinciding with the decline of the growth rate of the Polish economy. Changes in real wages by age groups, we see how they all have very similar trends.

---

30 The participation rate is defined as the total active population (employed and unemployed) over the working age population(16 to 64).

Table 1: Number of Poles Abroad

	Stock	Change	Flow	Population share
	in thousands	%	in thousands	%
1994	192.472			0.79
1995	185.389	-3.7	-7.083	0.74
1996	153.227	-17.3	-32.162	0.61
1997	139.805	-8.8	-13.422	0.55
1998	127.515	-8.8	-12.290	0.50
1999	133.247	4.5	5.733	0.51
2000	146.656	10.1	13.408	0.56
2001	191.166	30.4	44.511	0.72
2002	199.418	4.3	8.251	0.76
2003	229.833	15.3	30.416	0.87
2004	288.444	25.5	58.610	1.08
2005	343.884	19.2	55.440	1.29
2006	477.664	38.9	133.780	1.77
2007	626.927	31.2	149.263	2.29
2008	590.658	-5.8	-36.269	2.17

Source: Polish LFS

Note: In the first column we report the stock of working age (15-65) emigrants in each year, in the second column the percentage change in the stock with respect to the previous year, in the third column the flow of emigrants, given by the difference in the stock of the year with the previous year. Column 4 is the share emigrants in the total working age (15-65) population.

Table 2: Regional variation

Regions	Share of Emigrants		% Germany		% USA		% UK		% Ireland	
	1998	2007	1998	2007	1998	2007	1998	2007	2001	2007
Lower Silesian	0.2%	2.8%	40%	26%	12%	2%	14%	37%	2%	15%
Kuyavian-Pomeranian	0.2%	1.8%	52%	12%	0%	4%	0%	43%	0%	16%
Lublin	0.7%	3.1%	11%	10%	23%	5%	1%	37%	0%	8%
Lubusz	0.4%	2.1%	55%	35%	0%	2%	0%	21%	0%	19%
Łódkie	0.2%	1.4%	22%	11%	14%	5%	17%	46%	0%	9%
Lesser Poland	1.5%	3.5%	18%	15%	41%	12%	4%	29%	1%	10%
Masovian	0.4%	0.9%	20%	0%	36%	6%	6%	54%	10%	10%
Opole	0.7%	3.6%	86%	39%	8%	0%	0%	9%	0%	12%
Subcarpathian	1.7%	5.6%	7%	10%	46%	19%	3%	22%	0%	12%
Podlaskie	1.7%	3.1%	14%	17%	49%	16%	5%	34%	0%	4%
Pomeranian	0.4%	2.1%	50%	22%	4%	0%	14%	34%	0%	18%
Silesian	0.2%	1.5%	51%	17%	5%	2%	12%	39%	0%	7%
Swietokrzyskie	0.5%	3.6%	46%	20%	9%	3%	0%	34%	0%	9%
Warmian-Masurian	0.5%	2.1%	55%	22%	6%	2%	4%	34%	3%	13%
Greater Poland	0.2%	1.6%	67%	18%	9%	1%	0%	28%	0%	24%
West Pomeranian	0.3%	2.5%	38%	16%	9%	2%	0%	29%	0%	10%
Poland	0.5%	2.4%	27%	18%	29%	6%	5%	31%	1%	12%

Source: Polish LFS

Note: The share of emigrants is the ratio of working age (15-65) emigrants to the total working age population ine each region in 1998 and 2007. The other columns represent the percentage of emigrant in each region going respectively to Germany, the USA, the UK and Ireland in 1998 and 2007.

Table 3: Average Age, Gender Ratio and Education in 1998 and 2007 for Non-Emigrants and Emigrants

	Total Population		Emigrants	
	1998	2007	1998	2007
Age	38.1	38.6	34.0	32.3
% females	51%	51%	42%	34%
Education:				
% low	29%	14%	12%	5%
% intermediate	60%	67%	74%	76%
% high	11%	19%	13%	20%
% of 25-40 old	30%	32%	47%	54%

Source: Polish LFS

Note: Entries are the average age, percentage of females, educational distribution, and the share of individuals aged 25 to 40 for the total population and emigrants in the working age 15-65 for both sexes in 1998 and 2007. Low educated are individuals who have at most lower secondary education, or up to 8 years of schooling. Intermediate educated are individuals with secondary education, or between 9 and 13 years of schooling. High educated are individuals with individuals with post-secondary or tertiary education, or more than 13 years of schooling.

Table 4: Emigrant Education by Destination Country

	% total emigrants	Education low	Education intermediate	Education high	Average age
Germany					
all emigrants					
1998	27%	11%	78%	11%	33
2007	18%	7%	82%	11%	37
recent emigrants					
1998	36%	11%	77%	12%	32
2007	16%	7%	80%	12%	35
UK					
all emigrants					
1998	5%	10%	67%	23%	26
2007	31%	4%	71%	26%	29
recent emigrants					
1998	6%	16%	75%	9%	25
2007	37%	4%	71%	25%	28
USA					
all emigrants					
1998	29%	16%	74%	10%	39
2007	6%	3%	77%	19%	40
recent emigrants					
1998	15%	13%	72%	15%	32
2007	3%	2%	71%	26%	34
Ireland					
all emigrants					
1998	0%	0%	0%	0%	0
2007	12%	2%	72%	26%	30
recent emigrants					
1998	0%	0%	0%	0%	0
2007	12%	2%	70%	28%	29
Europe					
all emigrants					
1998	55%	11%	78%	11%	31
2007	84%	5%	77%	17%	32
recent emigrants					
1998	73%	10%	80%	10%	30
2007	88%	5%	76%	19%	31

Source: Polish LFS

Note: We report the share of all emigrants and the share of recent emigrants (those who emigrated within the last year) for Germany, UK, USA, Ireland and Europe (EU27) in 1998 and 2007 in the first column. In columns 2-4 we report the distribution of education for those two groups in 1998 and 2007 and in the last column we report the average age in the two groups in 1998 and 2007. Emigrants are in the working age (15-65).

Table 5: Probability to have one or more emigrant in the household on some household characteristics

	Probability at least 1 emigrant (1)		Probability at least 1 emigrant (2)		Probability at least 1 emigrant (3)		Household Descriptives			
							Emigrant		Non-Emigrant	
							mean	sd	mean	sd
Standardized HH earnings	-0.002***	0.0003	0.0003	0.0003	-0.002***	0.0003	2.43	0.99	2.47	1.01
Household Size	0.015***	0.0002	0.014***	0.0002	0.015***	0.0002	3.41	1.28	2.48	1.17
Share of Intermediate	0.022***	0.0011			0.023***	0.0011	0.70	0.29	0.62	0.38
Share of High	0.026***	0.0013			0.027***	0.0013	0.15	0.26	0.15	0.30
Share of women	0.004***	0.0012	0.005***	0.0012	0.004***	0.0012	0.50	0.21	0.52	0.27
Average Age/100	0.018***	0.0035	0.014***	0.0035	0.016***	0.0034	37.17	6.61	40.40	10.55
Share of Employed	0.020***	0.0014	0.021***	0.0014			0.85	0.33	0.85	0.30
N of observations	281782		281782		281782		5359		276423	

Source: Polish LFS

Note: * indicates significance at 10%, ** indicates significance at 5%, *** indicates significance at 1% level. In the three columns we estimate the probability to have at least one emigrant in the household. In column 2 we do not control for share of intermediate and high educated in the household. In column 3 we do not control for the share of employed older than 25 in the household. We control for regional and year and quarter fixed effects. Household earnings are standardized by the regional standard deviation of earnings over the period. The average is computed on the number of members who receive a salary. Household size is the number of people in the household. Share of education is the percentage of household members with that level of education within the household. Share of employed aged 25 is the percentage of employed older than 25 (to avoid including individuals who are still in education) in the household. All the variables, excluding earnings and the share of employed, are computed including the emigrant(s) in the average.

Table 6: Descriptive Statistics

Variables	Mean	Std. Dev.	Variables	Mean	Std. Dev.
Non-Emigrants			**Emigrants**		
			share of emigrants	1.2%	1.0%
% female	51%	1%	% female	40%	11%
age	38.3	0.5	age	33.0	2.4
intermediate/low educated	3.0	1.1	intermediate/low educated	12.8	10.2
high/low educated	0.7	0.3	high/low educated	3.0	3.3
Net Wages			**Net Wages**		
log average	6.99	0.06	log average	6.95	0.34
log average low ed.	6.74	0.09	log average low ed.	6.40	1.72
log average intermediate ed.	6.94	0.59	log average intermediate ed.	6.55	1.45
log average high ed.	7.23	0.08	log average high ed.	6.62	1.39

Source: Polish LFS

Note: We report pooled means and standard deviations for all regions and years (1998 to 2007). Entries are the percentage of females, the age, share of intermediate and high educated over low educated, real net average wage and real net wages by education group for non-emigrants. For emigrants we also report the share of emigrants over the total population. The sample of emigrants we use to report wages are the emigrants we observe before they emigrate and for whom we have labour markets information (see paragrph 2.3). Real wages are at 2008 prices. Non-emigrants

Table 7: Estimates for the relative growth of non-emigrants on relative growth of emigrants by education

	low	intermediate	high
relative share emigrants in low education	-1.648* (0.943)		
population growth of low ed. non-emigrants in t-1	-0.148* (0.089)		
relative share emigrants in intermediate ed.		-0.886 (0.947)	
population growth of interm. ed. non-emigrants in t-1		-0.160* (0.081)	
relative share emigrants in high ed.			0.705 (0.777)
population growth of high ed. non-emigrants in t-1			-0.045 (0.085)
Year dummies	Yes	Yes	Yes
Regional dummies	Yes	Yes	Yes
Other controls	Yes	Yes	Yes
R-squared	0.658	0.382	0.24
obs	160	160	160

Source: Polish LFS

*Note: Entries in this table are regression coefficients where the dependent variable is the relative growth rate of the non-emigrant population in the low, intermediate and high education group on the relative growth of emigrants in the same education group for years 1998-2007. We control for the lag of the dependent variable and for regional and year dummies. "Other controls" include the regional population growth in t and in t-1. Standard errors are reported in parentheses. * indicates significance at 10%, ** indicates significance at 5%, *** indicates significance at 1% level.*

Table 8: Zloty Exchange Rates with respect to USA Dollar, British Pound and Euro

	PNL/$	PNL/€	PNL/£
1998	3.48	3.9	5.76
1999	3.97	4.23	6.42
2000	4.35	4	6.58
2001	4.09	3.66	5.89
2002	4.08	3.84	6.11
2003	3.89	4.39	6.35
2004	3.66	4.54	6.7
2005	3.24	4.02	5.88
2006	3.1	3.89	5.71
2007	2.77	3.79	5.54

Source: Polish National Bank, statistics on exchange rates [1] and for 1992 OECD StatExtracts: PPS and Exchange rates (USD monthly averages) [2] and authors' calculations.

[1] *Exchange rates archive*

[2] *Exchanges rates are collected from the IMF publication "International Financial Statistics" and refer to IMF series "rf": year average national currency per U.S. dollars.*

Table 9: Effects of Emigration on Log Mean Wages, OLS and IV

Dependent variable	Net wages			
	OLS		IV	
	(1)	(2)	(3)	(4)
average	0.969*	0.999*	0.968*	1.011*
	(0.551)	(0.558)	(0.556)	(0.561)
low	-1.154	-2.138	-1.19	-2.155
	(1.510)	(1.463)	(1.522)	(1.472)
intermediate	1.285**	1.403**	1.304**	1.431**
	(0.569)	(0.569)	(0.574)	(0.572)
high	1.515*	1.142	1.537*	1.156
	(0.861)	(0.871)	(0.868)	(0.876)
(Adjusted) Partial R-squared			0.92	0.93
F-statistics for excluded			12.27	10.21
Year dummies	Yes	Yes	Yes	Yes
Other controls	No	Yes	No	Yes
obs	160	160	160	160

Note: Entries are estimated regression coefficients of the ratio of emigrants over the total population on log average net wages and on log average wages by education group for years 1998-2007. All regressions include region fixed effects. The IV is annual growth rate of real wages below the 40th percentile in country j (USA, UK and Germany) and wages in the construction and manufacturing sector for Ireland, expressed in zloty interacted with regional dummies. "Other controls": log regional population, mean regional age and gender, share of intermediate educated and high over low educated. Newey-West standard errors using 1 lag are reported in parenthesis. * indicates signifcance at 10%, ** indicates significance at 5%, *** indicates significance at 1% level.

Table 10: Effects of Emigration on Log Mean Wages, OLS and IV

	A		B		C		D	
	Gross Wages		Imputed Wages		Adjusting for Single Households		Residual wages	
Dependent variable	OLS (1)	IV (2)	OLS (1)	IV (2)	OLS (1)	IV (2)	OLS (1)	IV (2)
average	1.100*	1.116*	0.860*	0.871*	0.897*	0.918*	0.810*	0.817*
	(0.596)	(0.600)	(0.518)	(0.521)	(0.532)	(0.538)	(0.467)	(0.471)
low	-2.762	-2.771	-2.023	-2.029	-2.570*	-2.567*	-0.186	-0.155
	(1.728)	(1.738)	(1.287)	(1.295)	(1.386)	(1.400)	(1.236)	(1.245)
intermediate	1.619***	1.654***	1.201**	1.228**	1.148**	1.182**	1.227**	1.257**
	(0.614)	(0.617)	(0.562)	(0.565)	(0.547)	(0.553)	(0.523)	(0.527)
high	1.254	1.266	1.037	1.046	1.527*	1.535*	0.87	0.844
	(0.918)	(0.923)	(0.684)	(0.688)	(0.824)	(0.833)	(0.698)	(0.703)
(Adjusted) Partial R-squared		0.93		0.93		0.88		0.98
F-statistics for excluded		10.21		10.21		5.8		11.54
Year dummies	Yes	Yes	Yes	Yes	Yes	Yes	Yes	Yes
Other controls	Yes	Yes	Yes	Yes	Yes	Yes	Yes	Yes
obs	160	160	160	160	160	160	160	160

*Note: Entries are estimated regression coefficients of the ratio of emigrants over the total population on log average net wages and on log average wages by education group for years 1998-2007. In each panel we use a different measure of average, low, intermediate and high wages. In Panel A we reconstruct gross wages. In Panel B we impute wages for individuals who report to be employed but do not report wages. In Panel C we adjust the share of emigrants by the share of single households in the population. In Panel D, we use a two step procedure: for each year we firstly regress individual wages on educational dummies, age, age squared, gender and regional dummies and then we take the average regional log-wage residual (for the wages for each education group, we run the same regression explained above separately for education group). In both columns of Panel D in addition we control for the log of the regional population. All regressions include region fixed effects. The IV is annual growth rate of real wages below the 40th percentile in country j (USA, UK and Germany) and wages in the construction and manufacturing sector for Ireland, expressed in zloty interacted with regional dummies. "Other controls": log regional population, mean regional age and gender, share of intermediate educated and high over low educated. Newey-West standard errors using 1 lag are reported in parenthesis. * indicates significance at 10%, ** indicates significance at 5%, *** indicates significance at 1% level.*

Table 11: Effects of Emigration on Log Mean Wages, IV

Dependent variable	A GDP growth deviation		B Distance		C Mean Share	
	(1)	(2)	(1)	(2)	(1)	(2)
average	0.968*	1.014*	2.584*	1.686	2.068*	1.996*
	(0.561)	(0.565)	(1.562)	(1.337)	(1.136)	(1.158)
low	-1.165	-2.151	1.635	-1.938	-0.007	-1.348
	(1.536)	(1.482)	(4.229)	(3.506)	(3.083)	(3.008)
intermediate	1.301**	1.449**	2.857*	2.281*	3.388***	3.561***
	(0.579)	(0.577)	(1.601)	(1.363)	(1.208)	(1.220)
high	1.407	1.026	1.075	0.894	0.887	0.356
	(0.876)	(0.883)	(2.378)	(2.086)	(1.758)	(1.796)
(Adjusted) Partial R-squared	0.85	0.85	0.13	0.17	0.24	0.24
F-statistics for excluded	7.29	6.43	2.06	2.82	4.43	4.24
Year dummies	Yes	Yes	Yes	Yes	Yes	Yes
Other controls	No	Yes	No	Yes	No	Yes
obs	160	160	160	160	160	160

Note: Entries are estimated regression coefficients using different instrumental variables for the share of emigrants over the total population for years 1998-2007. In Panel A we use the GDP growth deviation and we interact regional dummies with the deviation of the GDP growth of destination country j from the OECD mean GDP growth (in US constant dollars). In Panel B, we interact the mean wage growth at the 40th percentile by the inverse of the distance of the regional capital from the capital of the country of destination. In Panel C, we interact a mean regional share of emigrant in destination country j with the wage growth in the same destination country j. "Other controls": log regional population, mean regional age and gender, share of intermediate educated and high over low educated. Newey-West standard errors using 1 lag are reported in parenthesis. * indicates signifcance at 10%, ** indicates significance at 5%, *** indicates significance at 1% level.

Table A1: Stock of emigrants by destination country and year

	Germany	Usa	Great Britain	Ireland	Italy	Spain	France	Netherlands	Belgium	Sweden	Austria	Other
1994	32%	26%	2%	0%	7%	2%	3%	2%	2%	1%	4%	18%
1995	32%	26%	3%	0%	9%	3%	5%	1%	2%	0%	4%	15%
1996	30%	28%	3%	0%	8%	3%	5%	1%	2%	1%	4%	16%
1997	28%	32%	3%	0%	8%	3%	4%	1%	2%	0%	2%	16%
1998	27%	30%	4%	0%	11%	2%	4%	1%	2%	0%	3%	16%
1999	28%	28%	4%	0%	13%	3%	3%	1%	4%	0%	3%	13%
2000	36%	22%	6%	0%	7%	2%	4%	2%	3%	0%	4%	13%
2001	37%	21%	6%	1%	11%	2%	4%	3%	4%	1%	3%	8%
2002	35%	22%	6%	1%	12%	2%	3%	3%	4%	1%	2%	8%
2003	31%	19%	9%	1%	13%	3%	5%	5%	4%	1%	2%	7%
2004	27%	18%	14%	2%	13%	4%	5%	3%	2%	1%	3%	7%
2005	22%	13%	23%	6%	11%	4%	4%	3%	2%	2%	2%	8%
2006	18%	9%	32%	9%	7%	3%	3%	3%	2%	2%	2%	10%
2007	16%	6%	33%	12%	7%	3%	3%	5%	1%	1%	2%	10%
2008	15%	6%	33%	11%	6%	4%	3%	6%	2%	2%	2%	10%

Source: Polish LFS

Note: We report for each year the share of emigrants over the total number of emigrants in that year going to one of these destination countries.

Figure 1: Total Number of Emigrants, from 1994 to 2008, in thousands

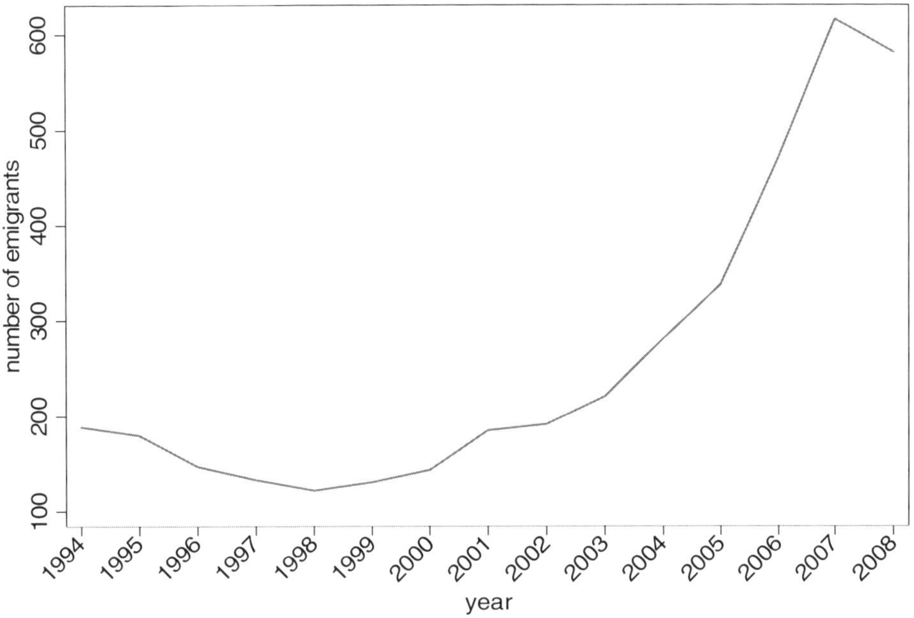

Source: Polish LFS
Note: Total stock of Poles residing abroad. Average of the quarters over each year

Figure 2: Number of Poles abroad from the Polish LFS and other datasets, a comparison

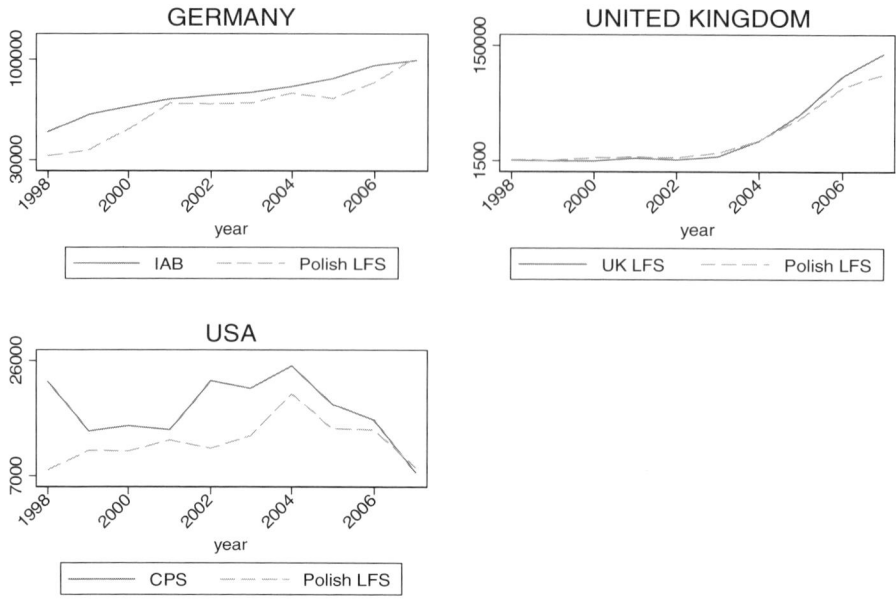

Note: For each destination country, we report the stock of Polish immigrants between 1998 and 2007. For the UK and USA we have information on the year of arrival in the country, so that we can report just recent immigrants (in the country for less than one year). For Germany we report all Polish immigrants. We smooth estimates in the USA by taking a moving average over a three year period (t-1, t, t+1), in each year.

Figure 3: Emigrants and total population: shares in each education group

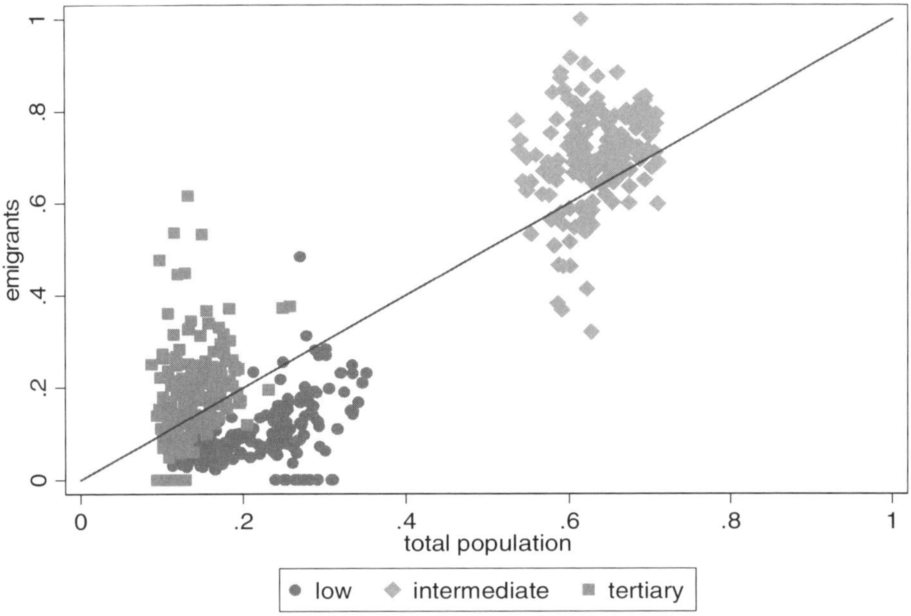

Source: Polish LFS
Note: The figure plots for each region and year the proprtion of emigrants in each education group out of total working age (15-65) emigrants versus the proprtion of total working age population in each education group.
Years 1998-2007.

Figure 4: Distribution of wage residuals for emigrants and non-emigrants

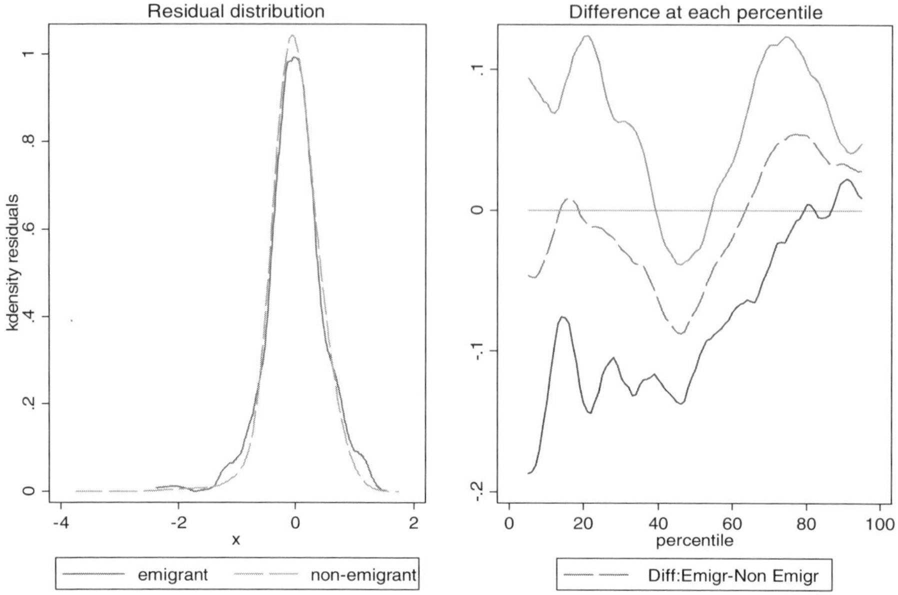

Source: Polish LFS
Note: On the left we plot the distribution of residuals for emigrants and for non-emigrants. On the right we plot the difference between emigrants and non-emigrants in the density of residuals at each percentile.

Figure 5: Polish emigrants in the destination countries' wage distribution

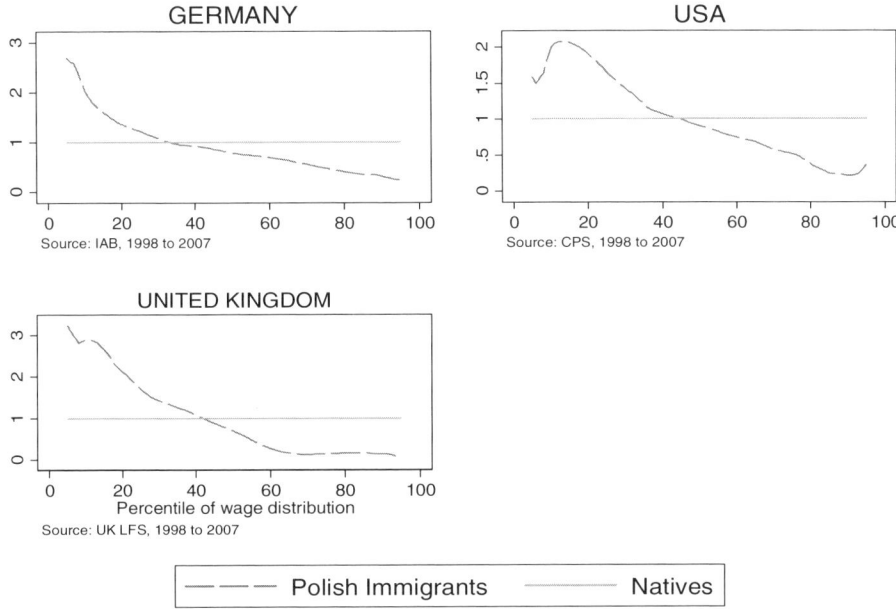

Note: In these graphs we report the relative distribution of Polish immigrant wages in the wage distribution of natives in Germany, the US and the UK, for years 1998-2007 pooled, using data from the destination countries. For UK and USA the figures refer to recent immigrants (less than two years in the country), for Germany the figure refers to all Polish emigrants.

Figure 6: Pre-2004 first stage coefficients and emigrant share by destination country and region

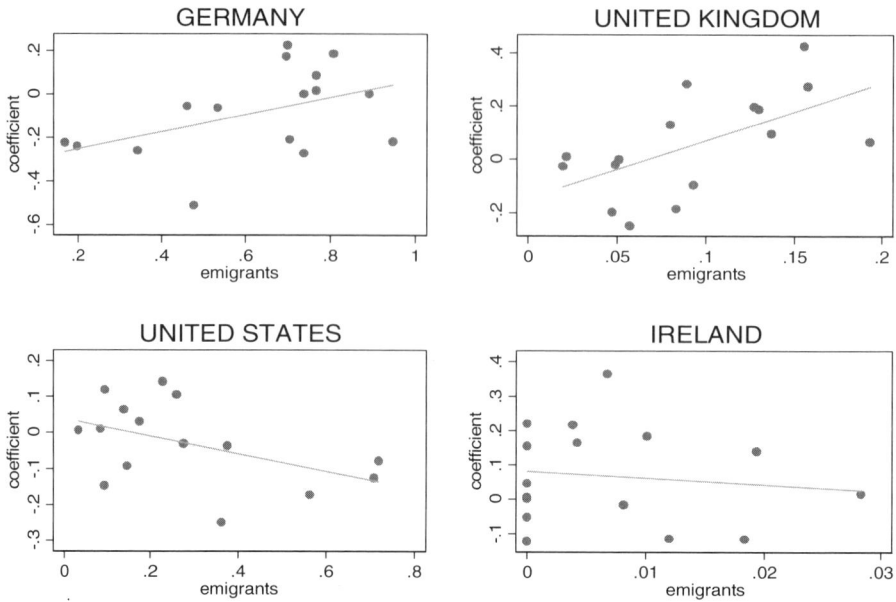

Source: Polish LFS
Note: In each panel of the graph we plot the first stage coefficient pre-2004 for each region versus the mean share of emigrants in the same region. The measure of emigrants we use is the average percentage of emigrants in the region to the destination country between 1998 and 2004 (excluded).

Figure 7: Post-2004 first stage coefficients and emigrant share by destination country and region

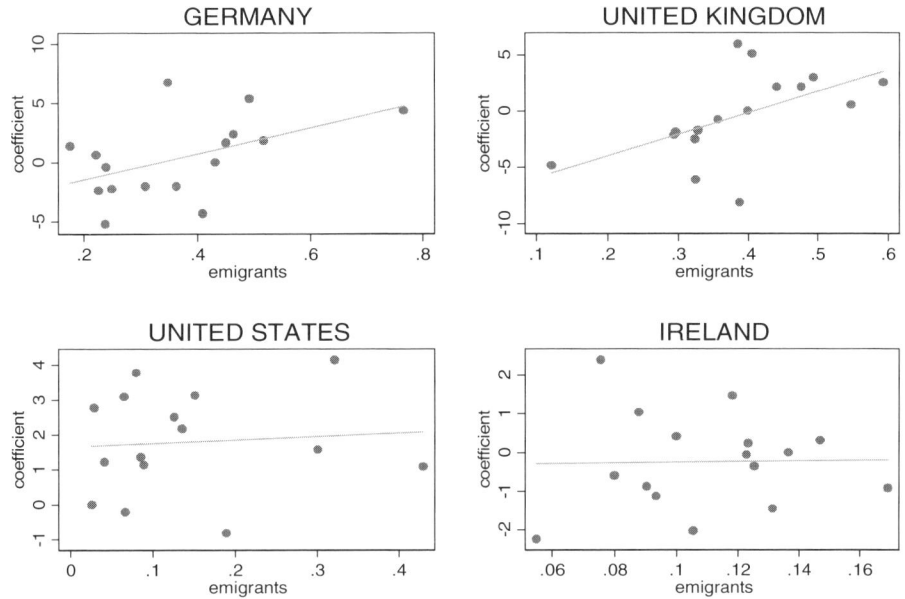

Source: Polish LFS
Note: In each panel of the graph we plot the first stage coefficient post-2004 for each region versus the mean share of emigrants in the same region. The measure of emigrants we use is the average percentage of emigrants in the region to the destination country between 2004 (included) and 2007.

Figure A1: Yearly Average Increase in Wages, 1998-2007

Source: Polish LFS
Note: Annual average increase in wages between 1998 and 2007

Figure A2: Yearly Average Increase in the Share of Emigrants (% points), 1998-2007

Source: Polish LFS
Note: Annual average increase in the share of emigrants (in percentage points) between 1998 and 2007.

Figure C1: Annual Real GDP Growth Rate

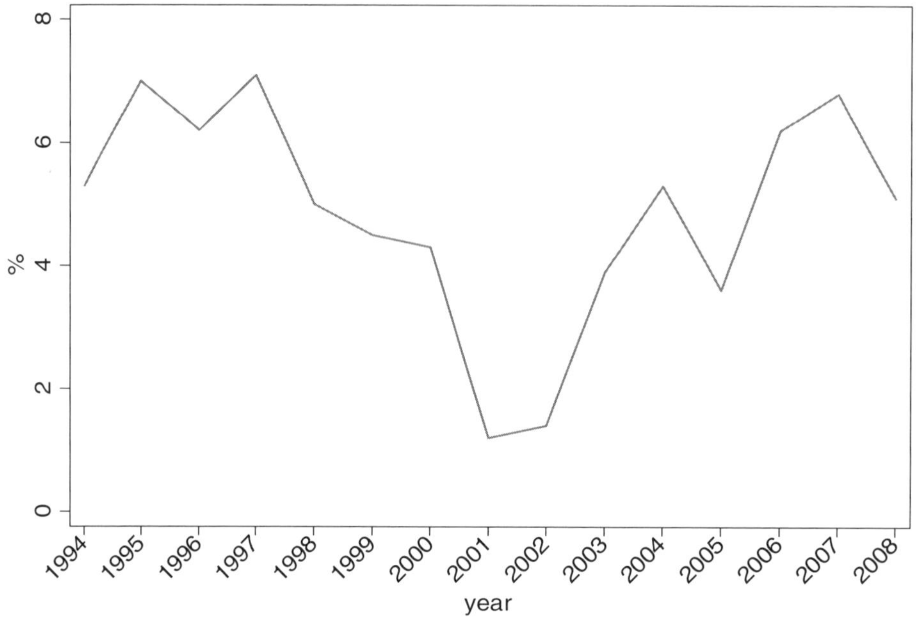

Source : GUS, Central Statistical Office, own calculations. GDP at constant prices (annual average prices of previous years)

Figure C2: Employment Rate in Poland, total and by education group

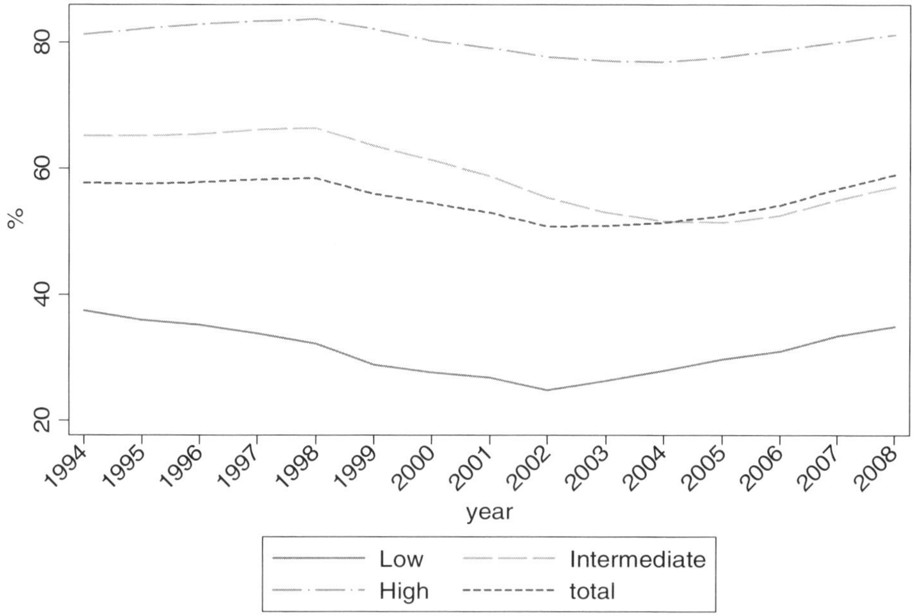

Source: Polish LFS
Note: The employment rate is defined as the number of employed over the working age population (15 to 65). Here we plot the employment rate for the total population (total) and by education groups (low, intermediate and high).

Figure C3: Real Wage Evolution, total and by age group (in logs)

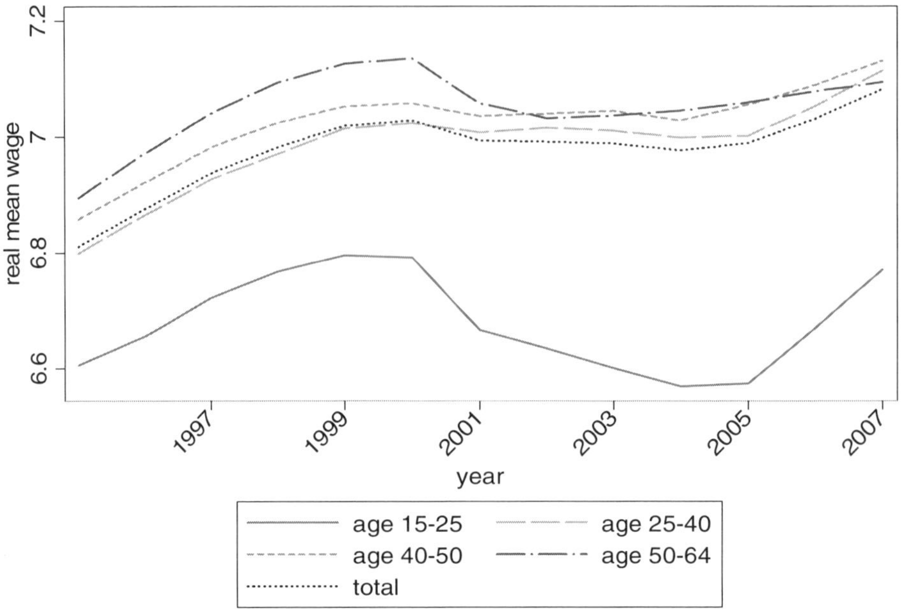

Source: Polish LFS
Note: The figure reports the evolution of log real mean wages in Poland, overall and by age groups over the years 1995-2007.
Real wages in 2008 prices.